STARTING

Continuum's *Starting with ...* series offers clear, concise and accessible introductions to the key thinkers in philosophy. The books explore and illuminate the roots of each philosopher's work and ideas, leading readers to a thorough understanding of the key influences and philosophical foundations from which his or her thought developed. Ideal for first-year students starting out in philosophy, the series will serve as the ideal companion to study of this fascinating subject.

Available now:

Starting with Berkeley, Nick Jones

Starting with Derrida, Sean Gaston

Starting with Descartes, C. G. Prado

Starting with Hegel, Craig B. Matarrese

Starting with Heidegger, Tom Greaves

Starting with Hobbes, George MacDonald Ross

Starting with Mill, John R. Fitzpatrick

Starting with Nietzsche, Ullrich Haase

Starting with Rousseau, James Delaney

Starting with Sartre, Gail Linsenbard

Forthcoming:

Starting with Hume, Charlotte R. Brown and William Edward Morris

Starting with Kant, Andrew Ward

Starting with Kierkegaard, Patrick Sheil

Starting with Locke, Greg Forster

Starting with Merleau-Ponty, Katherine Morris

Starting with Wittgenstein, Chon Tejedor

STARTING WITH LEIBNIZ

ROGER WOOLHOUSE
(University of York)

continuum

Continuum International Publishing Group
The Tower Building 80 Maiden Lane
11 York Road Suite 704
London SE1 7NX New York, NY 10038

www.continuumbooks.com

British Library Cataloguing-in-Publication Data
A catalogue record for this book is available from the British Library.

ISBN: HB: 978–1–8470–6203–1
PB: 978–1–8470–6204–8

Library of Congress Cataloging-in-Publication Data
Woolhouse, R. S.
Starting with Leibniz / Roger Woolhouse.
p. cm.
Includes bibliographical references and index.
ISBN 978-1-84706-203-1 – ISBN 978-1-84706-204-8 1. Leibniz,
Gottfried Wilhelm, Freiherr von, 1646–1716. I. Title.

B2598.W66 2010
193–dc22

2010011585

Typeset by RefineCatch Limited, Bungay, Suffolk
Printed and bound in Great Britain by
the MPG Books Group

CONTENTS

v

CONTENTS

ACKNOWLEDGEMENTS

The book has benefited greatly from the encouragement, help and comments of Glyn Barlett, Richard Francks, Paul Lodge, and of Shirley Woolhouse (to whom it is dedicated). They have undoubtedly improved it and corrected many mistakes, but they are not responsible for its faults or for any remaining mistakes.

INTRODUCTION

Starting with Leibniz begins with an account of the life, works and intellectual interests of the German philosopher Gottfried Leibniz (1646–1716). It then outlines what Bertrand Russell called Leibniz's 'fairy tale'. This 'tale' concerns elemental beings called 'monads' which form the basis of the world of our everyday experience. It was told by Leibniz in his *Monadology*, a short, popular synopsis of his philosophy which he wrote towards the end of his life. The following chapters aim to explain that philosophy. Focussing first on Leibniz's ideas as they were during the 1680s, and often placing them against those of his predecessor, René Descartes (1596–1650), they discuss his thinking on 'substance'; material body, immaterial mind and their relationship; the 'mechanical philosophy': matter, and motion and its laws; the metaphysics of force; space; freedom; God and our relationship with him. The concluding chapter concerns Leibniz's infamous optimism, his doctrine that this is the best of all possible worlds.

CHAPTER 1

LIFE AND WORKS

Gottfried Wilhelm Leibniz was born on 1 July 1646 in Leipzig, where his father was professor of moral philosophy. Between the ages of 15 and 21 he studied philosophy and jurisprudence at university, first in Leipzig and then in Altdorf. Following his Doctorate in Law at Altdorf he was invited to teach there, but he decided against this. He was, he enigmatically said, 'headed in an entirely different direction'. Whatever it was he had had in mind, he was, by 1668, at the age of 24, in Mainz in the service of the Elector, Johann von Schönborn, and one of his ministers, Baron von Boineburg. Besides an appointment as a judge, Leibniz worked in the capacity of librarian and adviser on foreign affairs. One of the diplomatic projects on which he was engaged by Boineburg concerned the election of the King of Poland. Another, which led to his spending a very important four-year period (1672–1676) in Paris, had the aim of diverting the attentions of Louis XIV, King of France, away from northern Europe by suggesting a plan for the invasion of Egypt.

Besides his involvement with affairs of state these years saw the development of Leibniz the writer, thinker and philosopher. His association with Boineborg led to the composition of a number of legal and jurisprudential pieces, and to the preparation of an edition of a book by a sixteenth-century Italian philosopher, Nizolius. Two important letters he wrote to Jacob Thomasius, his old teacher at Leipzig, also date from this period. Aiming to show continuities between the classical Greek philosopher Aristotle and the leading philosophers of his own time, Leibniz broached themes which were to concern him throughout his life: the nature of body and matter, the nature of motion and the relation of these things to mind.

Also at about the same time, as a result of a study of Thomas Hobbes and Christiaan Huygens, he composed two treatises on motion and the laws governing collisions between bodies. Besides setting down these early ideas on natural philosophy, Leibniz also wrote various papers and letters on religious and theological topics: proofs of the existence of God, the immortality of the soul and the doctrine of the Trinity.

From the very start and throughout his life Leibniz had a deep-rooted desire for harmony and synthesis. He continually tried to reconcile differences by taking the best from opposing factions, or by showing that their disagreements were merely apparent. This desire expressed itself at various points in his theoretical philosophy, as for example in his letters to Thomasius. It lent a certain eclectic quality to his work in which he often strove to find germs of truth even in conflicting theories: towards the end of his life he wrote that he had found that 'most of the sects are right in a good part of what they propose, but not so much in what they deny' (L 655). It expresses itself too in his theological writings, which have political and social dimensions as well as purely religious ones.

What Leibniz hoped to achieve in his theological writings was not just an end to religious disagreement but also the promise of civil peace. The Thirty Years' War which had ended when he was aged two had at least initially been fought across the Catholic/Protestant divide of a fractured Christendom. Both in Leibniz's Germany (which was a collection of loosely knit states) and throughout Europe these differences still had political as well as strictly religious weight. Leibniz's abiding hope was to see a reunification of the various Christian churches and sects – in particular the Roman Catholic Church and the Protestant Lutheran Church, of which he was a member.

In order to achieve this practical reunification, Leibniz strove at various points throughout his life to minimize or to effect a reconciliation between doctrinal differences. In various writings he is to be found trying to work out theological principles which would be acceptable to all the main denominations, and he is to be found arguing that any difficulties in what he says are not unique to him, but rather are problems faced by and common to all.

During his association with Boineburg he began work on various doctrinal decisions of the Council of Trent (1545–1563), for example those regarding transubstantiation and multipresence (the simultaneous presence of Christ's body in all the places where the sacrament is being celebrated). His hope was to arrive at interpretations of these Catholic doctrines which would be acceptable to Protestants. They needed still to be acceptable to Catholics too, of course; and he and Boineburg intended, by relaying them through various powerful and politically influential intermediaries, to have them officially approved by Rome.

A crucial stage in the development of his ideas began when Leibniz left Mainz for Paris on the diplomatic mission to Louis XIV in 1672. Unfortunately, not many months after his arrival in France, Boineburg, his friend and patron, and then (early in 1673) the Elector, von Schönborn, died. For a time Leibniz was allowed by their successors to remain in Paris (which he did until 1676), occupied at least in part as tutor to Boineburg's son.

Paris was the unrivalled intellectual centre of Europe, and Leibniz's stay there was immensely important from the point of view of his intellectual development. He had been brought up in the tradition of Aristotelian scholasticism and was not yet very well acquainted with more recent philosophy and ideas. Besides deepening his knowledge by his reading, the brilliant young twenty-six-year-old had a direct exposure in Paris to some of the foremost philosophers and scientists of the time. He was able to learn at first hand their most recent ideas. He met the Catholic theologian and philosopher, Antoine Arnauld, with whom he must have discussed ecumenical possibilities. He came under the influence of Christiaan Huygens, about whom he had written in his earlier work on motion, and who guided him in mathematical studies. He met Nicolas Malebranche, another Catholic theologian and leading Cartesian philosopher, and on visits to London he met Robert Boyle, and other scientists of the recently formed Royal Society, to which he was elected.

Besides being concerned with various philosophical issues, Leibniz turned his mind to technological matters, such as designing a calculating machine, which he exhibited to the Royal Society in London. But perhaps the most significant of his scholarly work during this time in Paris was in mathematics. His great achievement in this area was the invention of the differential calculus. He had perfected this by 1676, at the age of 30, and was unfortunately to become embroiled in a priority dispute with Royal Society friends and supporters of Isaac Newton, who had been working on the same mathematical ideas at the same time.

Life in Paris, at the heart of European intellectual activity, with its frequent and regular first-hand encounters with people with whom he could usefully discuss his ideas, was exactly to Leibniz's liking. He was made a member of the French Academy of Sciences, and his dearest hope was to obtain a research position there, which would have enabled him to remain in Paris. But this was not forthcoming and he had no choice but to accept an invitation to enter the service of Duke Johann Friedrich in Hanover, as his librarian and adviser. So in 1676 he set out to return to Germany, to what he would have seen as the intellectual provinces.

The journey itself was nevertheless fruitful and immersed him even more in the world of learning. He travelled *via* London, where he cemented his relations with the Royal Society, and thence to Holland. Here he met the microscopists Jan Swammerdam and Antoni van Leeuwenhoek, and the philosopher Benedict Spinoza with whom he had a number of long conversations. All of these three had influence on Leibniz's developing ideas.

Leibniz reached Hanover towards the end of 1676. He was to be based there for forty years, more than half his life, which ended in 1716. His first employer there, Duke Johann Friedrich, died in 1679 and was succeeded by his brother Ernst August; he in turn was followed in 1698 by his son Georg Ludwig (the future King George I of England). Leibniz was employed by the Court in a number of ways, ways whose variety illustrates some of the breadth of his abilities: librarian, diplomat, mining engineer. But his main official task, which was to extend to the end of his life, was to compile a history of the house of Brunswick-Lüneburg. This task, with its search through archival records for materials, involved a lengthy journey (1687–1690) through Germany and Italy. Apart from his official duties he was able during his first years in Hanover to find time to work on mathematics, logic and scientific methodology. He also studied the philosophical systems of Descartes and of Spinoza; and his letters and notes on various aspects of these contain the seeds of what eventually became (from the mid-1680s) a mature philosophy. Moreover, the years from 1682 saw him become a regular contributor (mainly of mathematical papers, often critical of Descartes) to a newly founded German scholarly journal, the Latin language *Acta Eruditorum*.

But, by and large, Leibniz had had to exchange the heady intellectual life of Paris for the less stimulating life of the provincial

Hanover court. Some discussion of his philosophical ideas was possible with Duke Ernst August's wife, Duchess Sophie, and with her daughter Sophie Charlotte. Leibniz never married and his close relations with these women were very important to him on a personal and emotional level. Moreover, his friendship with Sophie Charlotte, who became Queen of Prussia in 1701, gave him the opportunity of contacts with foreign visitors to the Royal Court in Berlin.

For real discussion, however, with equals who shared his intellectual interests Leibniz had to fall back onto exchange of letters, exchange which was inevitably slow, sometimes being held up by war. His contact with the world of learning was very largely by the voluminous correspondence he had with numerous people, spread over Europe. His feeling of isolation from first-hand contact with that world can be seen from a letter he wrote in 1696:

> All my difficulties derive from the fact that I am not in a great city like Paris or London, which have a plethora of learned men from whom one can obtain instruction and assistance. For there is much that one cannot do by oneself. Here one finds hardly anyone with whom to talk; indeed, around here one is not regarded as a proper courtier if one speaks of learned matters, and without the Duchess one would discuss such things even less. (Quoted by Mates 1986: 23)

Boineburg's death, while Leibniz was in Paris, had robbed him of some politically influential support for his plans for Church reunification, and Duke Johann Freidrich's death in 1679 did the same. Fortuitously, in the course of dealing with some of the late Duke's affairs, Leibniz was led into correspondence with the Landgrave Ernst von Hessen-Rheinfels, a Catholic convert. He found in this an opportunity of restoring the impetus to his ecumenical plans.

The interest in Church reunification figured in the composition, in 1686, of what has become known as the *Discourse on Metaphysics*. This relatively extended, synoptic, and polished text, written when Leibniz was 40, is often taken to mark the beginning of maturity in his philosophical thinking. Though in one way it was the result of years of thought, the *Discourse* was also the product of a few spare moments. In January 1686 Leibniz was snowbound in a village near the Hartz mountains, where he was occupied with technological problems to do with the drainage of the Duke's silver mines.

'Being where for several days I had nothing to do', as he reported, he switched his mind completely, from mining engineering to composing a 'short discourse on metaphysics' (LA 11). In the *Discourse* can be found, in some form or other, most of the philosophical ideas for which Leibniz became famous. In its 37 sections it touches on many of the topics and the themes to which he was to recur throughout the rest of his life: the nature of God and of God's actions; the nature of created substances; natural philosophy and the nature of body; the relation between natural science and metaphysics; the relation between the mind and the body; the human understanding, the human will and our relation to God.

But the initial motivation of the work, the first fruit of his maturity, is Leibniz's ecumenicalism. The *Discourse* plainly embodies the intention to provide a religious foundation which all Christians could accept. '[F]ar from harming religion' the principles he worked out 'serve to confirm it' he said. They have a 'usefulness ... in matters of piety and religion'. Far superior to earlier theories they remove 'very great difficulties, inflaming souls with a divine love' (DM 32). Wanting some assurance that these ideas really were acceptable to the Catholic point of view, and knowing that Ernst von Hessen-Rhienfels shared his ambitions for Church unity, Leibniz sent him a summary, asking for it to be transmitted to Antoine Arnauld for his reaction. The fact that Arnauld did not have the full text of the *Discourse*, but only its section headings no doubt contributed to his being less sympathetic to it than Leibniz must have hoped. Arnauld found

> many things in these thoughts which alarm me, and which nearly all men, unless I am mistaken, will find so shocking that I do not see what can be the use of a document which it seems will be rejected by the whole world. (LA 15)

A lengthy correspondence followed, in the course of which Leibniz explained and developed his arguments. He planned to publish the *Discourse* together with this correspondence, but he never did.

Following the composition of the *Discourse* Leibniz continued to work on its ideas. An objection to an important principle in Descartes' physics, which was contained in section 17, was published in the *Acta Eruditorum* in 1686. His criticism of this very influential French philosopher of the previous generation excited some controversy; but, undeterred, Leibniz, during the next decade, developed out of his objection a new science, what he called 'dynamics', the science of force.

As Leibniz conceived it, his new physical science, which related to bodily motion, had philosophical dimensions, and there are very close connections between it and his metaphysics. These were briefly touched on in another contribution to the *Acta*, 'On the correction of metaphysics' (1694). Leibniz explained them in the French *Journal des Savants* the following year, in 'New system of the nature and the communication of substances, as well as the connection between the soul and body'. In this important article Leibniz, under the cloak of anonymity, made public for the first time most of the central ideas of the philosophy he had been working on for some time. 'I thought of this system several years ago', he said, and in publishing them in French rather than Latin he was aiming to find a larger audience for them. His intention, he said, was 'to test the water', to expose the outlines of his philosophy to the learned world in the hope of provoking discussion from which he might benefit:

> I have ventured to offer these meditations … mainly in order to benefit from the judgements of people who are enlightened in these matters, for it would be troublesome to seek out and consult individually all those who might be willing to give me advice – which I shall always be glad to receive, provided it shows a love of the truth, rather than a passion for preconceived opinions. (NS 10–11)

As Leibniz had hoped, his 'New system' excited considerable interest. It led to a number of exchanges, both in publications and in private letters, with scholars such as Pierre Bayle and Simon Foucher. There is no doubt that the exchanges he was involved in were a measure of the intrinsic interest of what he had presented to the public, but they were also a reflection of its obscurity, an obscurity which stemmed only partly from the brevity of his exposition.

The conversations Leibniz had had with Sophie Charlotte formed the basis of the only book-length work, *Essays on Theodicy*, which he published in 1710. Aimed at the educated public rather than the world of learning, it deals with the relation between faith and reason, with human freedom and divine foreknowledge, and explains how God's creation can nevertheless contain evil and imperfections. In large part it was an answer to the ideas of the religious sceptic Pierre Bayle, which Leibniz and Sophie Charlotte had often discussed; but the answer often involves exposition of the bases of Leibniz's wider philosophy, to which it makes appeal.

Towards the end of his life and in answer to requests from friends, Leibniz wrote two popular summaries of his ideas, the *Monadology* and the closely associated *Principles of Nature and Grace*. In his last years he also engaged in a lively correspondence concerning matters in Newton's natural philosophy with Samuel Clarke, a friend of Newton.

Leibniz's intellectual interests were as varied as his public activities. He worked on chemistry, Chinese history, geology, jurisprudence, mathematics, philology, physics, politics, and theology, besides many branches of philosophy. Besides his calculating machine he invented and constructed a new kind of watch with multiple balance wheels, and had ideas for submarines and air-jet propulsion. For years he nurtured the idea of a kind of 'universal encyclopedia', a grand systematizing of all knowledge; and this idea imbued his work on book-cataloguing, on logic and on a rational universal language. It underpinned his interest in the founding of learned societies and journals, too.

Leibniz was a prolific writer. In 1923 what is now the Deutsche Akademie der Wissenschaften began the project of editing and publishing all of his work. By now something over twenty large volumes have been produced, and it is expected that the task will take two more centuries to complete. Most of the material exists only in manuscript, for Leibniz's published output was not great. So as far as philosophy is concerned there is a dozen or so articles in learned journals, and the book of *Essays on Theodicy*. But among what he did not publish there is relatively finished works for which he is now remembered: *Discourse on Metaphysics* (1686), *New Essays on Human Understanding* (1704), *Principles of Nature and Grace* (1714), *Monadology* (1714). There is also a huge amount of material in the form of notes, drafts and letters from his philosophical correspondences.

The student of Leibniz's philosophy is faced with the fact that he never wrote (leave alone published) a *magnum opus*, an exposition of his ideas that was finished, comprehensive, and definitive. Moreover, the short articles and letters in which his ideas are typically found tend to vary in presentation and language, and even (according to Bertrand Russell) in content, to suit the audience and occasion. His two long works, the *Theodicy* and the *New Essays on Human Understanding*, are limited in their conception; the former deals largely with the problem of evil and is a response to Bayle, while the ideas in the latter are expressed as reactions to, and in an order dictated by the *Essay Concerning Human Understanding* (1690) of the English philosopher John Locke.

None of this is to say that Leibniz presents us with a ragbag, and that taken in themselves his ideas form only a disconnected and piecemeal collection. There are, as the following chapters show, many connections between and common themes in all of his work in the various branches of philosophy with which he dealt: epistemology, ethics, logic, metaphysics, philosophy of language, political philosophy, philosophy of religion, philosophy of science.

FURTHER READING

Ariew (1995) is a good chapter-length account of Leibniz's life and works; Aiton (1985) and Antognazza (2008) are comprehensive book-length biographies.

Leibniz's two late writings, *Principles of Nature and Grace* and the *Monadology* are systematic synopses of his philosophy. A case could be made for saying that it is these that should be read by someone who simply wants to read some Leibniz to get some feeling for what he is about, rather than to follow him at arm's length, in an explanatory book such as this. But though very readable, and beguilingly evocative of intriguing matters, they are highly compressed. In any case they should be supplemented by the *Discourse on Metaphysics* and the 'New system'. All these pieces, and others, can be found in the collections of Woolhouse and Francks (1998), and Ariew and Garber (1989).

CHAPTER 2

LEIBNIZ'S 'FAIRY TALE'

When Leibniz was nearing 70 he wrote two elegant, systematic summaries of his philosophy, *Principles of Nature and Grace* and the *Monadology*. They were intended as accessible, popular accounts of his ideas; and, indeed, anyone who has heard the name 'Leibniz' has probably heard also of the world of 'monads' which these essays describe. It is a world which has provoked some dismissive reactions. In the eighteenth century Immanuel Kant described it as 'a sort of enchanted world' (Kant 1804: 375). At the beginning of the twentieth century Bertrand Russell echoed Kant, for he reported that when he first read it the *Monadology* struck him as a 'kind of fantastic fairy tale' (Russell 1900: xiii). It is easy to see why.

The world, Leibniz tells us, consists of 'monads'. These simple, shapeless, partless substances, are the true elements or atoms of nature. Being partless and without composition they have no beginning by any natural process of generation, or by some re-arrangement of already existing things, nor can they come to an end by any natural process of dissolution. They can only begin by creation or end by annihilation. In fact, 'they last as long as the universe, which will be changed but not destroyed' (PNG 2). Their lack of composition also means that monads cannot be changed or altered by any other created thing. As Leibniz strikingly says of them, they 'have no windows, through which anything could enter or leave' (Mon 7).

But this simplicity, this lack of composition, does not mean that there is no multiplicity or change in their internal qualities and actions. A monad must have qualities in order to be a being at all, and to be distinguishable from other monads and from itself at different times. In fact no two monads are perfectly alike and each monad is subject to continual change, change which, because of their 'windowless' nature, is brought about from within.

Specifically, a monad's qualities and internal actions are 'perceptions' and 'appetitions'. 'Appetite' is a tendency to move from one transitory perception to another. As for 'perceiving', it is not the same as being conscious, and some monads are as it were in a permanent stupor, with perceptions but with no consciousness or memory of them. They are, Leibniz says, something like *souls*, except that that term is improperly applied to them. It should be reserved for monads which are conscious, and have distinct perceptions, and memories of previous perceptions. Some of these higher monads are also able to reason, know necessary truths, do science and mathematics, and have a knowledge of themselves and of God. Leibniz calls monads of this third type, *rational souls* or *minds*.

Perception, as a purely internal activity of a 'windowless' monad, does not involve any direct interaction with other monads. It nevertheless, thanks to a pre-established harmony between its perceptions and those of other monads, 'represents' the external monadic multitude which makes up the rest of the created world. This multitude is infinite. The world is full, Leibniz said: there are monads 'everywhere' (PNG 3).

In internally representing this infinite multitude each monad is therefore 'a perpetual living mirror of the universe' (Mon 56):

> [J]ust as the same town looked at from different sides appears completely different, and as if multiplied in perspective, so through the infinite number of simple substances, it is as if there were so many different universes, which nevertheless are only perspectives on a single universe, according to the different point of view of each monad. (Mon 57)

So monads, of whatever kind, have 'a self-sufficiency' (Mon 18). 'Windowless', with nothing 'entering or leaving', they are 'the sources of their internal actions' – their perceptions and appetites (Mon 18). Moreover, they incorporate within themselves a representation of what these internal actions will be. '[T]he present is big with the future, what is to come could be read in the past … The beauty of the universe could be read in each soul, could one unravel all its folds which develop perceptibly only with time' (PNG 13).

This world of harmoniously connected monads has been created by a necessarily existing being, a being which has 'the reason of its existence within itself' (PNG 8). This originating, primal substance, or God, is omnipotent, omniscient and supremely good. The created world was not the only possible world however, for in the ideas of God is an infinite number of different possible universes. There must, then, have been a reason which sufficiently explains why he chose to create the one he did. This is that it was the best and most harmonious of all the possibilities – it manifested the greatest variety together with the greatest order. '[E]verything is regulated in things once for all with as much order and agreement as possible, since supreme wisdom and goodness cannot act without perfect harmony' (PNG 13).

A sort of fantasy this may indeed seem, but what Leibniz was intending to describe was not some fictitious imaginary world, but the underlying reality of *our* world. His monads are 'the true atoms' of our world. But how can the world he begins by describing, a world of monads, or simple partless substances, be the world we know, our world of flesh and blood human beings, of animals, of trees and flowers, and of rocks? We can begin to see how (though the matter is hardly obvious and straightforward, and still with some fairy-tale air), when he goes on to tell us that besides simple substances there are composite substances, collections of simple substances. Every simple substance 'forms the centre of a compound substance', and is the principle of its unity (PNG 3). The infinity of monads which surround that central monad form a mass which is its body. The two together are a living thing or creature. Where the central monad is a mind, it and its body constitute a human or some higher being such as an angel; where it is a non-rational soul it is an animal or a plant, or some more primitive life form.

In this way the monads form 'a world of creatures, living things, animals' (Mon 66). In fact, because every simple substance is the centre of a collection of other simple substances, there are worlds within worlds. There is a world of living things 'in the smallest portion of matter' (Mon 66). '[E]ach living body has a dominant entelechy, which in an animal is the soul; but the members of this living body are full of other living things, plants, animals, each of which also has its entelechy, or its dominant soul' (Mon 70):

[E]ach portion of matter can be conceived ... as a pond full of fishes. [E]ach member of an animal, each drop of its humours is also ... such a pond. And although the ... water which is between the fish of the pond, [is] neither plants nor fish, yet [it] also contain[s] plants and fishes, but most often so minute as so be imperceptible to us. (Mon 67–8)

The mass or portion of matter which is a soul's body is not assigned to it for ever. Though a simple, partless substance cannot be destroyed by any natural process, a composite substance can. Indeed 'all bodies are in a perpetual state of flux like rivers, and parts enter them and leave them continually' (Mon 71). But though its body might be subject to change, a soul is never without a body; there are no 'entirely *separated souls* or spirits without bodies' (Mon 72). Only God is completely detached from matter. What we call births or generations are 'developments and growths' from pre-formed seeds, what we call deaths are 'envelopments and diminutions' (Mon 73).

The harmony that there is between the perceptions of different simple substances extends to there being a harmony between the dominant monadic soul of an animal and the mass of monads which are its body. The union of the soul with the body is a matter of there being a conformity, a pre-established harmony between the two. 'The soul follows its own laws and the body likewise follows its own laws; and they agree with each other in virtue of the harmony pre-established among substances, since they are all representations of the same universe' (Mon 78). Souls and bodies have no direct influence on each other. '[B]odies act as if ... there were no souls, and souls act as if there were no bodies'. Yet, because they are in mutual harmony, 'both act as if each influenced the other' (Mon 81).

Though soul and body act in mutual harmony, the laws they each follow are of different kinds. Souls act according to the laws of final causes, of ends and means, of good and evil. Bodies act according to the mechanical laws of efficient causes, the laws which govern the movements of physical bodies.

In having perceptions which 'represent a multitude' (Mon 14) of other monads, souls in general are, as we have seen, 'living mirrors or images of the universe' (Mon 83). But minds in particular are also 'images of the divinity', the creator of the world (Mon 83). Besides representing the whole universe in their perceptions, they are able, Leibniz says, to 'imitate it' in that they can acquire scientific knowledge of it. They are able to come to an understanding of the system of the universe, by their discovery of the sciences of weight, measure, and number, by which God has ordered things. The rational soul or mind 'imitates in its own sphere, and in the little world in which it is allowed to act, what God performs in the great world' (PNG 14). In thus 'imitating' God's works, recreating them, so to speak, by reaching a rational understanding of them, minds are 'images' of God. This means that they 'enter into a kind of society with God' (Mon 84). It means that God is to them not just, as he is to other of his creatures, like an inventor to his machines. He is, rather, as a prince to his subjects or a father to his children.

As such, all rational minds are members of the City of God, the most perfect possible state ruled by the most perfect monarch. This city is a moral world within the natural world. It is in it that God's glory is most truly manifested. The natural world, in being the best possible creation, embodies God's greatness and goodness. But the members of the city of God, rational minds, are able to know and admire that greatness and goodness.

In this moral realm, this kingdom of grace as Leibniz calls it, 'there is no crime without punishment, no good action without proportionate reward, and finally as much virtue and happiness as is possible' (PNG 15). These rewards and punishments may not occur immediately, and reason cannot tell us in detail about what awaits us. But it can tell us that things have been arranged in this most perfect and satisfactory way. Such justice is achieved, 'not by any derangement of nature'; God has no need to interfere directly to punish and reward. It is achieved 'through the actual order of natural things, by virtue of the harmony pre-established from all time between the realms of nature and of grace, between God as Architect and God as Monarch' (PNG 15).

God is the most perfect and therefore the most lovable of substances, and love of him is a love which gives the greatest pleasure of which we are capable. If we understood the universe well enough we would see that 'it exceeds all the wishes of the wisest'. It is impossible it should be better than it is, 'not only for the whole in general but also for ourselves in particular' – at least so long as we are dedicated to God and love him (Mon 90). He is not only the designer and cause of our being, but also our master, who must be the goal of our wills. It is he who 'alone can produce our happiness' (Mon 90).

As remarked earlier, when Bertrand Russell, the great English philosopher of the first half of the last century, first read about all of this it struck him as a 'kind of fantastic fairy tale' – 'coherent perhaps, but wholly arbitrary' (Russell 1900: xiii). He knew, of course, that, however it might appear, Leibniz was not presenting a piece of fiction. The world of the monads was not a free-floating construct of creative imagination, but was intended as some kind of account of what constituted the reality of our world. Indeed, as he went on to say, 'a flood of light was thrown on all the inmost recesses of Leibniz's philosophical edifice' when he then read Leibniz's *Discourse on Metaphysics* and the correspondence he had concerning it with Antoine Arnauld.

The *Discourse* is an important product of what is described as Leibniz's 'middle period', the period at which the ideas he retained for the rest of his life (and finally outlined in the later works which Russell first read) began to reach some kind of maturity. It is undoubtedly true that it is through it (along with other works) that the 'fairy tale' of the *Monadology* can be interpreted and understood. The aim of the following chapters is to come to this understanding. Throughout them, we will need to bear in mind a complicating factor which Russell does not bring out. Leibniz's 'philosophical edifice', as Russell called it, has a temporal dimension to it. Though the ideas of his 'middle' period are continuous with those that came later, there are, over time, developments, and differences of accent and stress. The 'monads', for example, did not make an appearance by name, until 1696, yet, as will be explained in the following chapters, they are pre-figured much earlier.

FURTHER READING

The *Principles of Nature and Grace* and the *Monadology* are readily available in many collections, such as Woolhouse and Francks (1998), Ariew and Garber (1989), Parkinson and Morris (1973).

CHAPTER 3

SUBSTANCES

i. SUBSTANCE: ITS GENERAL CHARACTERISTICS

Central to Leibniz's 'fairy tale' are 'monads'. These 'simple substances' are, he said, the ultimate constituents of reality. He did not speak of 'monads' as such until the 1690s, but they are, effectively, descendants of certain mind- or soul-like 'entelechies' which occur earlier.

The notion of 'substance' was the crucially important metaphysical category for Leibniz. It is, he wrote towards the end of his life, 'of the greatest importance and fruitfulness for philosophy' (NE 150). So much is this so that, when properly understood and analyzed, there can be seen to follow from it 'most of the important truths about God, the soul and the nature of body, which are generally either unknown or unproved' (WF 32).

The notion played a central role not just in Leibniz's thinking; it was important for his immediate predecessors too in what is known as the 'early modern period' of philosophy. Unfortunately, in Leibniz's view, the Frenchman René Descartes (1596–1650) and the Dutch philosopher Benedict Spinoza (1632–1677) failed to understand the true nature of substance; a failure which led directly to what he saw as Descartes' 'errors' and Spinoza's 'paradoxes'.

At the bottom of much of what these seventeenth-century philosophers said about substance is what the Greek philosopher Aristotle (384–322 B.C.) had said centuries before. As Aristotle introduced it, an account of substance is an account of 'being' (the Greek word 'ousia', which is translated 'substance', derives from the Greek verb for 'to be'). He focussed on what was, he said, a perennial and much disputed question, 'what is being, what is substance?'. One way to understand this question, a way which fits both much of what Aristotle said and what later philosophers said, is to hear it as asking 'What is reality; what does reality ultimately consist in?'. There are, however, two ways of taking this. We might take it to be the question '*Which* things are real? What are the basic constituents of ultimate reality? What are examples of substances?'. Or we might take it to be the question 'What are the criteria for something's being substantial and real? What is it about the basic constituents of reality that their reality consists in? What is it that makes them the ultimate realities, and other things somehow non-ultimate and dependent on them?'.

The early Greek philosophers gave various answers to the question understood in the first of these ways. According to Epicurus (341–270 B.C.) the basic substantial constituents of reality were material atoms; according to Thales (c. 624–c. 546 B.C.) water was the one thing which was ultimately real, all else was reducible to it. Among Aristotle's examples of substances were living animals. In Leibniz's case, the answer was twofold, for, as we saw in the 'fairy tale', his metaphysical scheme contained both 'simple' and 'composite' substances. The first are the mind-like entities which he called, variously, 'entelechies', 'forms', 'monads'. Together with a body they make up a 'compound' substance, a living animal. '[E]ach simple substance or distinct monad ... forms the centre of a compound substance (e.g of an animal)' (PNG 3).

These two kinds of substances will be looked at in detail when we have considered Leibniz's answer to the question understood in the second way, as a request for the criteria for something's being real and substantial. A very basic criterion, both in the Aristotelian tradition and for Leibniz, was *independence*. Substances are independent of and underlie other things; things which are not substances are in some way dependent on substances. The notion of independence allows of some flexibility as to its exact meaning; and at different times it has been given different interpretations (sometimes in the writings of the same philosopher). But those meanings are all echoes of Aristotle's original teaching.

Substance, Aristotle taught, is that which is the subject of predicates and is not the predicate of anything else. 'Substances', he said, 'are most properly so called, because they underlie and are the subjects of everything else' (Aristotle 1941: 2b39). So the man Alexander and the horse Bucephalus are the subjects of predicates, as for example when we say of Alexander that he is healthy or of Bucephalus that he is lame; and, unlike their health and lameness, the man and the horse are not predicates of anything else. Put slightly differently, a substance is not a dependent state or property (a 'mode' or 'accident') of something else. Alexander and Bucephalus have independent being, unlike their health and lameness which do not exist apart from them and which depend on them for their existence. Health and lameness are simply states or ways of being of the subjects to which they are attributed.

Related to the idea of substances as subjects, and underscoring the idea of their being independent, is the idea that they are what undergo or underlie change. Aristotle called this 'the most distinctive mark of substance' (Aristotle 1941: 4a10). One and the same substance can retain its identity while admitting contrary qualities through time. Alexander did not cease to be Alexander when he became unhealthy; Bucephalus was Bucephalus, lame or not.

All of this is something Leibniz accepted. Using traditional scholastic vocabulary, he described substance as 'ens per se', 'being through itself', not dependent on anything else for its existence. In many places he aligned himself with this Aristotelian tradition according to which substances are *independent*, basic realities, self-subsistent beings, which exist in their own right – unlike their properties or states.

A further feature of substantiality for Leibniz was *unity*. The reality which God created consists basically of *individual* substances. He referred to substances not merely as 'unities', but as 'truly single beings' (LA 118). In doing so he was making a contrast between, in traditional terminology, a *'unum per se'*, a unity in itself, such as a sheep, as contrasted with a *'unum per accidens'* or an *'ens per aggregationem'*, an accidental unity or aggregated being, such as a flock of sheep, or a chunk of marble.

The notion of substance was one topic pursued at length in Leibniz's correspondence with Antoine Arnauld which concerned the *Discourse on Metaphysics*. Arnauld felt that Leibniz's definition of substance in terms of unity, besides not being in accord with common usage, was rather arbitrary and lacked any good rationale. He thought that substances should be defined in the straightforward Aristotelian way, simply as subjects, as things which were not properties, nor modes or ways of being of anything else. Given this understanding, Arnauld said, a block of marble or a flock of sheep would count as substances, and he thought it paradoxical of Leibniz to say that there is nothing substantial in them. But, as Leibniz pointed out, he was not out of the way in requiring substances to be unities; the distinction between *per se* unities and accidental or aggregated beings was drawn from the scholastic Aristotelian tradition. Moreover, even the common conception of substances as independent beings would lead to ruling a flock of sheep out as a substance: quite clearly, a flock has no existence independent of the sheep which compose it. In any case, he said, though they were not substances themselves, he did not deny that there is something substantial in a piece of marble or a flock of sheep. On the contrary, *anything which is not a substance*, such as the flock of sheep, *must presuppose something that is*. 'Any being by aggregation presupposes beings endowed with true unity, because it derives its reality ... from that of the things [the substances] which make it up' (LA 96).

Leibniz associated the *unity* or oneness of a substance with its being *indivisible* and *indestructible*. It is possible to see this idea as some kind of a metamorphosis or transmutation of the traditional idea that substances are what underlie and persist through change; but it goes much deeper than this. 'Substantial unity', Leibniz said, 'requires a complete indivisible being, which is indestructible by natural means' (LA 76). We might recall that these are characteristics of the 'fairy tale' monadic substances; and it is easy to see that they rule out the chunk of marble or the flock of sheep as being substances. Clearly these are divisible; the block can be broken up and the flock can be dispersed, and in being so they are divided and destroyed. It is not so obvious, however, that Alexander and Bucephalus could still count as substances, for surely they too can be torn apart and killed. What Leibniz had to say to this is something we will come to.

A further characteristic of Leibnizian substance, another which has its roots in tradition, is *activity*. Repeating the independence criterion, Leibniz said substance is 'being which subsists by itself', and then he continued, and '[b]eing which subsists by itself is that which has a principle of action within itself' (L 115), i.e. to be truly independent something has to be the cause of its own states. The centrality of activity in Leibniz's thinking about substance, throughout his life, can hardly be over-stressed; it and its ramifications are used, we shall see, to produce a highly distinctive theory of substance. In his middle period he remarked that the essence of substances is a 'primitive force of action' (L 155); and in later years he was still insisting that 'everything that acts is an individual substance, but also ... every individual substance acts without interruption' (NI 9).

ii. AGAINST CARTESIAN CORPOREAL SUBSTANCE

Much of what Leibniz said about 'substance' was in conscious and explicit disagreement with what Descartes had said. As for Leibniz, so for Descartes before him, substance is what is ultimately real and independent. Descartes found that there were two kinds of substance, two kinds of basic reality, two kinds of thing which, apart from their dependence on God, depend on nothing else for their existence. These two kinds were material, corporeal, bodily substance and incorporeal or mental substance. For each of these two kinds there is a principal property which defines or constitutes its essence or nature: material substance essentially is *extension*, a spreadoutness in length, breadth and depth; mental substance essentially is *thought*.

Descartes' idea that these two properties, extension and thought, define or pick out two kinds of *substance* is justified *via* the claim that they underlie other properties. Though some properties (such as being coloured, or globular) presuppose being extended, being extended, he said, presupposes no other property. Hence, it could be said, extended things are independent and depend on nothing else for their existence. Similarly, some properties (such as being angry) presuppose thought (which Descartes understood as mental activity in general); but thought itself presupposes nothing else – hence thinking things depend on nothing else for their existence. Since, in particular, extension does not presuppose thought, and thought does not presuppose extension, the two types of substance are exclusive.

Given corporeal substance as Descartes understood it, as a substance *whose defining property or essence is extension*, Leibniz was adamant in rejecting it. But in rejecting corporeal substance as *Descartes* understood it, he did not reject corporeal substance as such, even though he was perhaps never entirely easy with it. Perhaps the idea of corporeal substance was acceptable, so long as it was understood in some other way. Perhaps some other and satisfactory account could be given of substances which *are* corporeal and extended (such as human beings, or horses), *but whose essence or nature lies in something other than extension*. If no other account could be given then things such as pieces of marble or horses could not be taken to be genuine substances. What other account or accounts he gave is something we will come to. For the moment we need to look at Leibniz's reasons for rejecting corporeal substance as Descartes understood it, as a substance whose defining property or essence is extension.

One reason Leibniz had for rejecting the idea that the essence of a corporeal substance could be extension was his requirement that substances, of whatever kind, must be unified indivisible individuals. A quantity of extended matter cannot qualify here. It is forever divisible: as Descartes himself had said, 'however many parts a body is divided into, each of the parts can still be understood to be divisible' (CSM 1.202). So, to Leibniz's mind, the idea of an *individual, unified*, extended substance which is a substance *in virtue of its being extended* is incoherent. In his correspondence with Arnauld, Leibniz was quite clear that if Alexander and his horse are to count as substances then, though they are extended, their substantiality (which requires unified indivisibility) cannot consist in or derive from that, as Descartes would have held. '[I]f ... body is a substance, and not ... a being unified by accident or by aggregation, like a heap of stones, it cannot consist in extension' (LA 58). In fact he was quite confident that Alexander was a unified corporeal substance. How, despite his infinitely divisible extended body, this could be, we have yet to see.

Its infinite divisibility was not Leibniz's only reason for objecting to the idea that extension could constitute a substantial essence. Another depended on a thought which is a crucial and central element in his own positive account of substance: substances are, in a sense to be explained shortly, '*complete* beings', whereas '[e]xtension', he says, 'is an attribute which could never make up a complete being' (LA 72).

It is clear then that for Leibniz extension cannot be a substantial essence. Understood *as Descartes understands it*, corporeal substance is to be rejected. So *if* there are such substances, and Leibniz thought that there are, it cannot be *by virtue of* their extendedness that they are substances. Their substantiality must come from something additional to their being extended, something which, despite their being extended, gives them unity.

What, then, does Leibniz believe this 'additional something' is? Quite simply, it is something like the second of the two kinds of substance which Descartes distinguished – mental or thinking substance. The substantiality of a bodily corporeal substance results, Leibniz says, from its having in it 'something related to souls' (DM 12).

In contrast to what he felt about Cartesian corporeal substance, Leibniz was, broadly speaking, happy with Descartes' other category of substance, mental substance, a substance whose essence or nature Descartes supposed is thought. It is clear that problems concerning unity and indivisibility, which arose in the case of Cartesian corporeal substance, do not arise here. There was not, for Descartes, just 'mind stuff', as it were, but individual minds. Each person is, or has, a mind or soul. Leibniz knew that some people had held that there are no particularized minds or souls, and that there is some 'universal spirit', which 'thinks, believes and wills one thing in me but ... contrary things in different persons'. He thought that this is just wrong. Experience teaches us that 'we are in ourselves something particular which thinks, which perceives, and which wills, and that we are distinguished from another being who thinks and wills something else' (L 559).

Minds (or mind-like entities, souls, entelechies, forms, monads) are, then, substances for Leibniz. They are crucially important ones too, for they are the 'something' that is there in a corporeal bodily substance on account of which it is a substance. Without minds or souls there would be no extended corporeal substances. Anyone who thinks about the nature of substance, he said, will come to see that 'either bodies are not substances ... or that the whole nature of body does not consist solely in extension ... On the contrary, something related to souls which is commonly called a "substantial form" has necessarily to be recognized in them' (DM 12). We must now look at the thinking about the nature of substance which led Leibniz to this conclusion.

iii. COMPLETE CONCEPTS

Leibniz embraced the traditional Aristotelian idea that a substance is that which has predicates or attributes and is not the predicate or attribute of anything else. But as it stands this is a rather superficial explanation of what a substance is. It does not tell us what it is for a substance to have an attribute, and we must, he said, go deeper than this. We must consider what it is 'to be truly attributed to a particular subject' (DM 8).

Leibniz's conclusion was that, in general, a proposition which attributes a certain predicate to a subject ('Alexander is healthy' for example) is true, i.e. truly attributes that predicate (being healthy) to that subject (Alexander), 'when the predicate is ... included in the subject'. This inclusion is such, he continued, that 'whoever understood the notion of the subject perfectly would also judge that the predicate belongs to it' (DM 8). This theory of truth, that a proposition is true when and only when the predicate is contained in the notion of the subject, was something which Leibniz came to quite early on, and he was in no doubt about it. If this is not what truth is, he told Arnauld, 'then I do not know what ... is' (LA 56). Leibniz's confidence notwithstanding the theory is strikingly at odds with the more natural idea that truth consists in correspondence with the facts; and (as we shall have occasion to see) it seems to have the consequence that all truth is necessary truth.

Just why Leibniz held the theory has been a matter of some discussion; but what needs to be said here is that it was on the basis of it that he proposed a deeper account of what a substance is: 'an individual substance or complete being' is something which has a notion 'so complete as to include and entail all the predicates of the subject that notion is attributed to' (DM 8). An individual substance or complete being is not just, superficially, a subject of predicates. It is, more deeply, something which has a complete notion or concept which contains all the predicates of which it is the subject.

We need to look more closely at this idea that a substance is something with 'a complete concept'. We might note, first, that Leibniz spoke not only of individual substances as having *complete concepts*, but also of them as *complete beings*. This second characterization is in fact the more basic of the two. It is only because individual substances are complete beings that they have complete concepts.

By contrast, the concept of 'a king' is *not* the concept of an individual substance or complete being; it is *not* a complete concept. It is true that it includes all the things that can be predicated of someone (Alexander the Great, say) who is a king *in so far as he is a king*. But it does not involve everything which is true of that king. It does not involve all that the concept of Alexander involves. The concept of 'a king' is, he says, an 'abstraction'; it is not sufficiently determinate for an individual. The concept of a king is essentially open and not completely determinate. It is, of course, not completely *in*determinate; it does not leave it open whether kings are male. Kings *are* male, for it is part of the concept of a king that they are. But it does leave it open and undetermined whether (for example) kings have two children (some have, some have not), or (for example) are married (some are, some are not).

But Alexander himself was fully determinate. He was a complete being. Though his being a king did not determine them, there are determinate historical facts as to whether or not he had children and how many, and as to whether he married. He was not an incomplete abstraction (as though he were just 'a king', and nothing else). He was a concrete being which existed in space and time. In fact he was *completely* determinate: for *any* predicate which it would make sense to attribute to him (being six feet tall, dying from poison) there was a determinate truth about whether it held of him or not. Correspondingly, the concept of Alexander is a complete concept; it involves everything which was true of this fully determinate and complete individual.

It is not too difficult to go some of the way with Leibniz about this. We can accept that Alexander the Great was a complete, fully determinate individual; for we can easily accept that at his death there was a complete set of truths about him relating to every moment of his past life. We might easily also think of there being a complete concept involving all these truths. We are not in possession of that concept, of course. What we know of Alexander we know from history. It is only from written records that we know he died from poison. But the records are incomplete, and there are many things about him we do not know. Yet it is not too much of a stretch to think of God as knowing all these things, and that he is in possession of Alexander's complete concept.

We might find it less easy to accept, however, what Leibniz further holds, that Alexander was complete and fully determinate (or, at least, that he had a complete concept) *at his birth*. But it is part of Leibniz's scheme that his concept was in fact complete from the start, and that God from the outset sees in the individual notion of Alexander that he dies from poison.

iv. SOULS AND SUBSTANTIAL FORMS

As we have seen, Leibniz suggested that anyone who reflects on what he has said about individual substances as complete beings with complete concepts will see that substances therefore have in them something like a soul, something which is often called 'a substantial form'. How are we to understand this? What is the connection between being a complete individual substance with a complete concept, and having something like a soul or 'substantial form'?

Leibniz maintained that the individual corporeal substance Alexander was a complete being with a complete concept from the outset; his future was already 'closed' at his birth in that there was then a complete set of determinate truths about him, such as (to name just one) that he would die from poison. Following on from that, his thought seems to have been, there must have been something about Alexander at his birth which portended or presaged that he would die in that way. So, he concluded, 'there is in the soul of Alexander for all time ... marks of everything that will happen to him' (DM 8).

Properly understood, then, substances have complete concepts, and this involves their having something in them (a 'substantial form') akin to a mind or soul, which bears the marks and traces of all that is included in their complete concepts. There are two things that need to be further explained here. It is because of its mind or soul that a corporeal substance is a substance; the substantiality of corporeal substances derives from this. But, first, what are 'substantial forms'? And, second, exactly how do they account for the substantiality of corporeal substances?

Like so much else in seventeenth-century philosophy the doctrine of substantial forms had its roots in Aristotle. It flourished in the Middle Ages with Thomas Aquinas, and was taught by later scholastic philosophers and theologians. In fact it was one aspect of the scholastic tradition from which the 'new philosophers' of the early modern period distanced themselves. The so-called 'father of modern philosophy', Descartes, is particularly energetic in his rejection of it. But it is something which Leibniz, in his reconciling, ecumenical fashion, wished to save from the past. We will see in Chapter 6 that he forthrightly rejected the use of the doctrine in the context of the physical sciences. But, in the present context, he thought that it is only in terms of it that we can come to a proper understanding of corporeal substance. He recognized that he was 'proposing a big paradox' in reintroducing substantial forms when they had been 'all but banished'. But this needs to be done, he said, if we are to explain how there can be individual corporeal substances.

The doctrine of substantial forms portrays such substances as composites of *matter* and *form*. We could conceptualize a particular thing, a statue say, as a composite of matter, such as bronze, arranged in or according to a certain form, the form of a man. It was along some such lines that an individual substance, such as the horse Bucephalus, was understood to be a composite of matter (flesh, blood, bones), organized into a horse by means of the *substantial form* of a horse.

'Form' was not simply 'shape' however, as in the introductory example of the statue. The 'form' (or 'nature' or 'entelechy' as other terms have it) of an oak tree, say, is not just its visual shape. The form was supposed to ground the whole organization of the tree: its various parts, such as its leaves and bark, and their functions; its characteristic activities, such as growth by synthesizing water and other nutrients, and its production of fruit; its life cycle from fruit to fruit bearer. It is because it is organized and active in this way that the matter which constitutes an oak tree was thought to 'embody' or be 'informed' by the substantial form 'oak'. Accordingly, the oak's properties and activities, the things that are natural to it, were said to 'flow' or 'emanate' from its entelechy: 'a thing's characteristic operations derive from its substantial form' (Aquinas 1964: 3a.75, 76) Aquinas said.

So the doctrine of substantial forms conceived of an individual substance as active, 'embodying' in itself, as its 'nature', the principles of its development and change. To understand why an individual substance is as it is, and does as it does, is to understand how its properties and changing states 'flow' or 'emanate' from the nature, or form, of the kind of thing it is. 'There are', says a medieval commentary on Aristotle's *Physics*, 'individual and particular behaviours appropriate to each individual natural thing, as reasoning is to human beings, neighing to horses, heating to fire, and so on … [T]hese behaviours … arise from the substantial form' (quoted by Garber 1986: 129).

Living things were the prime examples of individual substances, of independent *entia per se*, and their substantial forms were called their 'souls'. Thus oak trees, horses, and human beings all had souls which caused and governed all their characteristic behaviours. If something had an oak tree soul it would live the characteristic life of oak trees.

Leibniz's 'complete concept' account of substance was the basis for his reintroduction of substantial forms, but it eventually dropped out of his thinking. Instead of 'complete concepts' and their derivation from a theory of truth, Leibniz began to think in more dynamical terms. He spoke of a 'law of the same series of changes, a series which it [a substance] traverses unhindered' (AG 173), and said that this 'inherent law' is a 'primitive force of acting' (NI 12). The association of substantial form with force and activity became more and more prominent; and 'active force' in fact became so basic in Leibniz's thought that, rather than seeing it as a feature of substantial form, he began to introduce and explain substantial form in terms of it. 'There must be found in corporeal substance ... a primitive motive force ... [T]his substantial principle itself is what is called *the soul* in living things and *the substantial form* in other things' (NI 11).

In his correspondence with Arnauld, Leibniz applied this so-called 'hylomorphic' analysis of individual material substances, their analysis into 'matter' (*hyle*, in Greek) and 'form' (*morphe*). He had no hesitation that this was the correct understanding of individual corporeal substances, and on the whole he was confident that human beings are such corporeal substances, with souls, or forms, and thought that if they were it was unlikely that other animals were not also. Indeed we will see in the next chapter that it is essential to his metaphysics that there are corporeal substances other than human beings.

He explained to Arnauld that a living human being is a composite of a rational soul, or substantial form, an entelechy, and an amount of material, flesh, blood and bones, which the form animates and organizes. What makes a human body into a living human is that its flesh, blood and bones are 'ensouled'. As such, a living human being is, of course, an *extended* material substance. But the crucial point is that its substantiality does not, as for Descartes, derive from its being material or extended, but from its being organized by a form.

Descartes saw a living human being as a *union of two substances*, mind and body, rather than as *one* substantial form and matter composite. Arnauld suggested the Cartesian view to Leibniz. Surely, he said, '[o]ur body and our soul are two substances which are really distinct' (LA 66); the soul therefore is not the substantial form of the other. Leibniz's reply was that 'our body in itself, or the *corpse*, considered in isolation from the soul, can only improperly be called *a substance*' (LA 75). Taken by itself, he made clear, the body is simply a mass of extended matter, and not a substance.

Though Leibniz did not say at this point whether, in isolation from the body the soul, the organizing form, can or cannot be correctly called a substance, we have already seen that he thought it can be. For Leibniz, as for Descartes, minds or souls taken by themselves are individual immaterial thinking substances. In this he diverged from traditional hylomorphism. Aquinas, with immortality in mind, had in fact allowed that the specifically rational part of human souls could exist apart from matter; but this did not fit well with the official teaching that neither matter nor form is a complete substance in its own right. But for Leibniz, souls or forms are, in and of themselves, incorporeal substances. *In a sense* this means that for Leibniz there *are* two substances to consider in thinking about a living flesh and blood human being. The living human is a corporeal material substance, and the animating form or soul is an incorporeal immaterial substance too. But only one of these, the soul, is akin to one of the pair of substances which for Descartes make up a living human being. The other is akin to the Cartesian pair. On Leibniz's scheme the Cartesian substantial body, the human being leaving the soul aside, is not a substance.

Given that Leibniz holds that immaterial souls are complete substances in their own right it might be natural to suppose that he also holds that they can actually exist apart from the body. As we will see in Chapter 8, Descartes believed that they could. Leibniz, however, did not. He held that there never are any forms which are not embodied in some matter, and so part of a corporeal substance: there is, he said 'naturally ... no soul without an animate body' (LA 124). What this means for his account of birth and death will be examined in Chapter 8.

v. COMPLETE WORLDS APART

Leibniz not only adopted the doctrine of hylomorphism according to which individual corporeal substances embody forms which organize and systematize their functions and activities, but also he extended it in significant ways. Traditional hylomorphism held that many of the characteristics of an individual substance arise from the form it embodies, but did not hold that *all* of them do. Its 'vegetative soul' was not thought to inform the whole of an individual oak's life. Many things were thought of as being 'accidental' to it – the exact number of acorns it happens to produce, say. However, having argued that individual substances are *complete* beings with *complete* concepts, so that what is true of a substance must be included in its

concept, Leibniz went on to say that its substantial form is responsible for *everything* that becomes true of the corporeal substance
which embodies it. Each substance 'contains in its nature the law of
the continuation of the series of its operations, and *everything* that
has ever happened to it or will happen' (LA 136, italics added).
Furthermore, many of the things which traditional hylomorphism considered 'accidental' were thought of as coming about
as a result of the tree's being passive with respect to some *external* cause. The number of its leaves at a given time would be attributed partly to the wind which had stripped some away. Moreover,
though the oak's form was supposed to govern the synthesizing of
water and other nutrients, these materials still needed to be provided
to it from outside. However Leibniz's belief that a substance contains in its nature *everything* that happens to it, means that all of
these things 'come from its *own* depths' (LA 136), from an 'internal
principle' (Mon 11). This means (to underscore the point) that
for Leibniz nothing happens to a substance as a result of external causes. External causes cannot, he said, 'influence it internally'
(Mon 11). A substance is, that it is to say, 'windowless'. On the
face of it this is a rather extraordinary idea (if we remember that
Alexander the Great and his horse are substances). We will examine
it in more detail later.

Yet another, perhaps an even more extraordinary, way in which
Leibniz extended the traditional doctrine was to claim that each
substance 'expresses' the entire universe. Each monad, in Leibniz's
'fairy tale', is 'a perpetual living mirror of the universe' (Mon 56).
This further extension seems in entirely the opposite direction from
those just discussed. On the one hand Leibniz has told us that substances are completely isolated from each other; everything about a
substance becomes true of it out of its own depths; external causes
do not influence it. Everything that happens to a substance 'is a
consequence of its ... being ... [I]t is completely protect[ed] from all
external things ... and, with God, suffices to itself' (DM 32). On the
other hand we now find that substances are in some way utterly connected with each other, they each 'express', even if only confusedly,
the entire universe. The soul of Alexander contains not only marks
of everything that will happen *to him*, but 'even traces of everything
happening in the universe' (DM 8). 'The beauty of the universe',
Leibniz says, 'could be read in each soul, could one unravel its folds
which develop perceptibly only with time' (PNG 13).

The account Leibniz has now given of individual substances provides an answer to a question which he raised at the outset of the *Discourse on Metaphysics*. Where does the boundary lie between God's actions and those of created things? As he pointed out, there are different views about this. Some people, he says with Descartes in mind, think that God 'does no more than conserve the force He has given to creatures' while others (Malebranche, one of Descartes' followers) think that God 'does everything' (DM 8). What Leibniz has said about substance amounts to a resounding rejection of the second of these views. God does *not* do everything, Leibniz held. For, quite to the contrary, there is in individual created substances 'a self-sufficiency which makes them the sources of their internal actions' (Mon 18). All the changes that happen to created substances and the predicates that become true of them are a development of their own 'natures' or 'forms'.

This does not mean that God does nothing. As Leibniz said, substances are self-sufficient '*except* for ... dependence upon God' (LA 136, italics added). Unlike God they are not necessarily existing beings. So God is nevertheless responsible for initially creating them with their forms and natures; and he is also responsible for sustaining them. God 'conserves' created substances and indeed 'even continually produces them by a kind of emanation' (DM 14). But this 'continual production' is definitely not any weakening of the idea that all that happens to a substance 'comes from its own depths', as the development of its form. Leibniz explained to Arnauld that

> everything that happens to a substance is in consequence of the first state God gave to it when he created it, and, leaving aside extraordinary concourse, his ordinary concourse is just a matter of preserving the substance itself in conformity with its previous state and the changes that carries. (LA 115)

The distinction Leibniz made here between God's ordinary and extraordinary concourse was originally a scholastic distinction and a seventeenth-century commonplace. According to it, those philosophers who believe God does everything, believe in God's extraordinary concourse in all things. They believe, as Leibniz explains, that God regularly acts on substances in some way 'otherwise than merely in keeping each substance on its course and following the laws established for it' (LA 58).

Leibniz's 'fairy tale' (as we will see in detail in Chapter 10), gives an answer to the question which might arise here as to why God created the world he did. In God's mind is an array of possible worlds, each populated by possible individual substances, each with its complete concept; and, in short, out of these possible worlds, he chooses the best which, in his goodness, he creates.

Now the idea that God chose to create a certain possible world of individual substances, each with its complete concept, can be expanded in more than one way. Let us suppose the actually chosen world was one in which the first man sinned on the tenth day. We can now ask: what was it *on creation day* that made the now actual world *that* one, and not some other possible world, in which the first man never sins? Certainly Leibniz would not have thought it a sufficient answer simply to appeal to the complete concepts in the mind of God of the substances in the world. Complete concepts in God's mind are simply an account of the content of his plans and wishes. What carries them out or executes them? We have supposed that the world God wanted or planned was one in which the first man sins on the tenth day, but Leibniz was keen to focus on the question of how God's plans or wishes for the world get executed. One answer might be that God carries them out. In this case, what it was on creation day that made it the world it was and not some other, was that *God's intentions* were to bring about that man's tenth-day sin himself, which, because it did not arise naturally from what God had already created would be an act of 'extraordinary concourse'. To think of all events and changes in the world in this way would be to 'believe that God does everything'.

As mentioned, Leibniz had his contemporary Malebranche in mind as someone who believes that 'God does everything'. Such a belief was part of what was called 'occasionalism'. Malebranche and others made a distinction between 'real' or 'active' causation on the one hand, and 'occasional' causation on the other, and held that God alone is a real or active cause. According to them, in the created world there are only 'occasional' causes, and all change in that world comes about from God's activity. When a stationary body moves after a collision, the real cause of its motion is not the fact that a moving body came into contact with it; that is just the 'occasion' for the motion. The real cause is God.

Quite clearly Leibniz did not agree with this 'occasionalist' account about God's dealings with the world. It runs counter to his idea that individual created substances have 'a self-sufficiency' (Mon 18), that they are themselves active, and in ways governed by their own natures or forms. According to this, what *on creation day* made it that the chosen world was one in which the first man would sin, was not that on that day God's intentions were to bring about that man's later sin. It was rather that at his creation the man was the 'embodiment' of a certain complete concept, a 'form', whose development over time would bring about his later sin. Though the 'ordinary concourse' of God 'sustains them in their course', substances are responsible themselves for what they do. When the occasionalists, 'who believe God does everything', deny activity to created substances, they are, in Leibniz's eyes, in fact robbing substances of their substantiality. A *substance* has a form; it has 'a principle of action within itself' (L 115). The view that created things are not substances, and that there is no substance other than God (so that God and the world are identified), was explicitly held by Leibniz's near contemporary, Spinoza. Leibniz was quick to draw the parallel. Occasionalism, he said

> seems with Spinoza to make of God the very nature of things, while created things disappear into mere modifications of the one divine substance, since that which does not act, which lacks active force ... can in no way be a substance (NI 15).

In holding that everything that happens to a substance happens to it from its own depths, Leibniz was therefore in significant disagreement with an occasionalist such as Malebranche. But, as we saw above, this idea has the corollary that 'an external cause cannot influence it [a substance] internally' (Mon 11). It involves, that is to say, the denial of any interaction or causation *between* substances. This consequent idea, however, constitutes an agreement between the two sides. For if, as 'Malebranche' held, there is no real causation or activity within the created world, it follows that there is no causation or activity *between substances* in the world. The 'occasionalist' view of causality and Leibniz's opposition to it is something to be explored further in Chapter 7.

vi. SUBSTANTIAL FORMS AGAIN

Leibniz rejected the Cartesian account of corporeal substance as something whose essence was extension. It was, it will be remembered, the fact that extension could not provide the indivisibility and natural indestructibility Leibniz required of true substantial unity, which led him to introduce substantial forms. He argued that the embodiment of an indivisible indestructible substantial form in extended matter would result in an indivisible indestructible corporeal substance. Arnauld questioned Leibniz about all of this.

When a marble tile is broken into two, what happens to its substantial form, Arnauld asked. Leibniz's straightforward response was that a tile is *not* a corporeal substance, and so has no substantial form. It does not have the kind of unity, a unity *per se*, which a corporeal substance must have. A tile is like a heap of stones, merely a 'being by aggregation' (LA 72). Like a ring with diamonds set in it, like fish in a frozen pond, like a flock of bound sheep or a chain of links, it has only accidental and not substantial unity. It has no substantial form. Certainly there are differences in these cases as to the degree of cohesion of their parts. But, no matter how close or tight, mere physical connection does not produce anything more than accidental unity. Even machines, whose parts 'work together to the same end' (LA 101) are not substantial unities. Their unity 'depends on the inventions of our minds' (LA 76); Leibniz 'attributes substantial forms only to corporeal substances that are more than mechanically united' (LA 77).

But how, in the case of a genuine corporeal substance, something which is 'more than mechanically united', does the substantial form produce a unity? Leibniz did not have much to say about this. It is quite clear that he held that the immaterial form taken by itself is an indivisible unity. He took this to be a traditional view, and Arnauld had no difficulty with it. It is quite clear too that the result of the embodiment in matter of that indivisible form is supposed to be a unified indivisible corporeal substance. All that Leibniz had to say in support of this idea is that we know that this is so from our own case. We know that 'man is a being whose soul gives him a real unity, despite the fact that the mass of his body is divided' (LA 120). The fact that a human body is divided into various parts, organs and limbs, does not count against the living person's being a unity, nor does the fact that a person might lose some of those parts.

Arnauld agreed that it was indeed true that corporeal human beings are indivisible unities. He pointed out that we cannot 'conceive of half a man' (LA 88) (though we can conceive of half of his body). But though he also agreed that their souls are indestructible he did not see how this could be so, as Leibniz thought, of the corporeal substances themselves. After all, even if the corporeal whole, the fleshly human being, is in some sense indivisible, it surely is not indestructible, it *does* come 'to an end when the soul is separated from the body' (LA 88). Leibniz's view, however, is that souls do not become separated from bodies at what we call 'death'. The death of an 'animated' corporeal substance is not a separation of soul from matter. What it is is a transformation rather than a dissolution of the corporeal substance. When a living animal is burnt, the fire transforms it and reduces it in size; it does not totally destroy it and separate its soul from its body. There is 'something animated even in ashes' (LA 122).

This will be discussed further in Chapter 8. What must be considered next is the status for Leibniz of the extended matter which forms the body of corporeal substances such as men, and other animals and insects. This itself will throw light on the idea that corporeal animated substances are indestructible and on 'death' are transformed into 'small organised bodies produced by a kind of contraction from larger bodies which have decayed' (LA 122).

FURTHER READING

Mercer and Sleigh (1995) and, more extensively, Mercer (2001) give accounts of Leibniz's earlier, pre-'middle period', thought.

On the general characteristics of Leibnizian substance see Rutherford (1995a: 133–48), and for an extensive overall account of them see Parkinson (1965: ch. 5).

Adams (1994: 326–38), Garber (1995: 284–8), Nason (1946), Sleigh (1990a: 116), and Wilson (1989: sect. 16) discuss some of Leibniz's arguments against Cartesian substance.

Complete Concepts

Extended discussions of Leibniz's theory of truth can be found in Brody (1977), Jarrett (1978), Mercer and Sleigh (1995: 107–9), and Parkinson (1965: ch. 3). For further discussion of substances and their complete concepts see Broad (1975: 20–5), Fleming (1987), Ishiguro (1979b), Rutherford (1995a: 119–24, 138–46), Wiggins (1987). Rutherford (1995a: 148–54) discusses the move from a theory-of-truth based account of complete concepts to a dynamical theory.

Further reading on occasionalism is given at the end of Chapter 7.

CHAPTER 4

MATERIAL BODY

We saw in the last chapter that, having firmly rejected Descartes' view that extension could be the essence or nature of a substance, Leibniz proposed, in his 'middle period', that an individual corporeal substance is a unity consisting of the embodiment of a form, a soul, in some matter. The substantiality of a material substance, such as a human being, comes, he held, from its substantial form. He held also that the form, the soul, was itself a substance, but that the matter, the body, considered apart from the form, was not. But now if a human body, taken by itself and purely as a material thing, as a corpse or cadaver, is not a material *substance* then what *is* it? If it is not an independent substantial being, then it must in some way be dependent on substance. So what exactly is matter for Leibniz? In what way is it dependent on substance? How are we to understand the corporeality of corporeal substances?

Very broadly speaking it is possible to see two different views about this which Leibniz had, at different times. There was, at the time of his correspondence with Arnauld, and through what have been called his 'middle years' (1686–1703), what might be called a *realist* view; and there was an *idealist* view, held in his 'later years'. How accurate even this very broad picture is, and how it should be filled in detail, is one of the most discussed and disputed topics among Leibniz scholars. It may well be that elements of the later view can be found in the middle years; it may be that the earlier view was never really abandoned. But the broad picture will serve us here.

i. CORPOREAL SUBSTANCE REALISM

One of Leibniz's reasons for rejecting extended matter itself as a substance was the divisibility of extension, and therefore its inability to provide unity. Consequently, the human body, considered apart from the soul, is no different from any other non-substantial body, such as a heap of stones, or a piece of marble. All those things, Leibniz said, are aggregates, so-called 'accidental beings'. But what are aggregates *aggregates of*? One answer might be that extended non-substantial matter (whether a corpse or a marble tile) is an aggregate of smaller portions of extended matter. This would make those parts aggregates themselves of course. But now since 'every part of matter is actually divided into other parts ... and since that goes on and on in the same way, you will never arrive at something of which you can say it is a true being' (LA 77).

To Leibniz's mind this answer would be completely unsatisfactory. An extended material body, considered by itself and apart from any form, is not a real entity on its own account; it is merely an entity made up by aggregation. What reality it has it must get from its parts. '[B]eings by aggregation can have only as much reality as there is in their ingredients' (LA 72). But if its constituent parts are themselves aggregates (and so-on *ad infinitum*), there will be no reality to extended matter. What is required, then, is that an aggregate is an aggregate, not just of more matter, but of material *substances*. Aggregated extended matter, such as a corpse or a marble tile, has no independent reality as substance in its own right; so unless there are material substances that it depends on and of which it is an aggregate, it will have no reality at all. '[I]f there are no corporeal substances [for non-substantial aggregated beings to be aggregated from] ... then bodies will only be true phenomena, like the rainbow' (LA 77).

Arnauld suggested to Leibniz that perhaps the division of matter does not 'continue endlessly'. Perhaps it is not infinitely divisible; perhaps its division terminates in minute material atoms, still extended but perfectly hard and indivisible. Couldn't these indivisibles count as having substantial unity and reality, a reality from which larger bodies, aggregated out of them, could derive a dependent reality? Indeed, Arnauld pointed out, there were Cartesians, such as Gerauld de Cordemoy (d. 1684), who 'in order to find a unity in bodies, have denied that matter is infinitely divisible, and have asserted that we have to admit indivisible atoms' (LA 67). Descartes himself did not believe in material atoms, but he did not hold that 'unity' was an important characteristic of substance anyway.

Leibniz certainly approved of what he took Cordemoy's motives to be in introducing physically indivisible atoms – the desire to have some basic extended *substantial unity* out of which larger bodies could be aggregated. 'The excellent gentleman saw the truth' he said; but he saw it 'confusedly and through a cloud' (quoted Garber 1995: 96), and did not adequately explain it. For one thing, Leibniz thought, Cordemoy was quite wrong to believe in material atoms, things which he himself rejected.

Leibniz's basic thought, that non-substantial beings by aggregation must be aggregates of substances, seems correct enough in some cases. For example a non-substantial crowd is an aggregate of people, each of whom is a substance. Yet what of the body of one of those people, considered apart from their form as a non-substantial aggregate? It too, Leibniz insisted, 'is an aggregation of substances' (LA 135). But, what substances are these? How did he propose to satisfy the need for genuine substantial unities out of which material bodies such as human corpses, or marble tiles, can be aggregated?

His proposal is somewhat astonishing. All non-substantial matter, he said, whether marble tiles or human bodies, is divided into *small, animated, material substances*. A marble tile or human corpse is like a crowd of people, or flock of sheep, in being a collection of living animated material substances. But what of the matter which composes the bodies of these further substances? This too would be a mere phenomenon if it were not an aggregate of further smaller animated material substances. 'I think', Leibniz wrote to a correspondent, 'that there is no smallest animal or living being... whose body is not, in turn, divided into many substances' (AG 168). The matter of any animated corporeal substance is composed of other and smaller animated corporeal substances, and their matter is composed of still smaller animals, and so-onwards *ad infinitum*. Just as a living human being is a composite of form and matter, so its matter – its body taken by itself, apart from its form and merely as extended matter – is an aggregate of parts *which are themselves* animated substantial composites of form and matter:

> I accept that a body on its own, without a soul, has only a unity of aggregation; but the reality which it still possesses derives from the parts which make it up, and which retain their substantial unity because of the countless living bodies which are contained within them. (LA 100)

The substantial forms of the corporeal substances out of which all material aggregates are composed are not, of course, rational minds (except in some case such as a crowd of people). But, as we have seen already (in Chapter 3), Leibniz thinks there are different kinds of soul. Moreover, though it is clear where a crowd of people divides into individual people it will not always be clear just where other non-substantial material aggregates actually divide into corporeal substances. Where such divisions are is simply a matter of empirical fact. 'I hardly know how far ... flint should be divided so that organic bodies ... might occur; but I readily declare that our ignorance has no effect on nature' (AG 168).

This answer to the question as to the genuine material substantial unities out of which, Leibniz argued, non-substantial material aggregates must be composed is effectively a kind of fusion of his own hylomorphic living corporeal substances with Cordemoy's purely material atoms. For Descartes, who, like Leibniz, did not believe in material atoms, extended matter is continuous, homogeneous, potentially infinitely divisible. It has no ultimate parts. For Cordemoy, by contrast, it is actually divided into extended but indivisible atoms. It does have ultimate material parts. To an extent Leibniz agreed with Cordemoy: matter, Leibniz held, *is* actually divided into unitary parts, and sometimes, having in mind their indivisible unity, he called them 'atoms'. But these Leibnizian 'atoms' are not just matter; they are animated form/matter corporeal substances. To an extent Leibniz agreed with Descartes too. Just as Descartes thought matter is infinitely divisible into yet smaller and smaller material parts, so Leibniz thought it is actually infinitely divided into smaller and yet smaller animated corporeal substances. Every part of non-substantial extended matter is divided into corporeal substances: 'there is a virtually infinite number of animals in the smallest drop of water ... matter ... [is] filled throughout with animated substances' (LA 122).

ii. IDEALISM

According to the 'idealism', which, it is generally agreed, Leibniz held at any rate during his 'later years', substantial reality consists only of 'monads' or mind-like entities. '[C]onsidering the matter carefully, we must say that there is nothing in things but simple substances [monads], and in them, perception and appetite'

(AG 181). To what extent Leibniz's idealism in fact amounts to denying that there are any corporeal *substances*, or to what extent he wanted to continue to speak of such things, are topics of discussion among scholars. But in any case it was not part of his idealism to reject material body; within his idealism human beings, for example, still have bodies which have some kind of reality. However, they do not get it, as earlier, from being physical aggregates of corporeal substances, but in some other way, from monads. In fact Leibniz seems to have considered two different views about the status of bodies in a world which consists basically only of immaterial monads and their perceptions and appetitions.

iii. PHENOMENALISM

One view is closely related to what in recent times is known as *phenomenalism*. Though it is usually associated with the 'idealism' of his later years, Leibniz can be found toying with it during his middle years too, as a radical alternative to the 'corporeal substance realism' of that period.

According to it, the 'reality' of material bodies consists in agreement or harmony among monadic perceptions. Thus, Leibniz said, in the end all phenomena can be explained 'solely through the perceptions of monads functioning in harmony with each other, with corporeal substances rejected' (L 604). One contrast a view of this kind has is with indirect or representational realism. According to this there are two things involved in our perception of the material world: our subjective perceptions of that world, and that world itself, existing independently of our perceptions of it. Naturally there is considerable agreement between the subjective perceptions of different perceivers, and between those of the same perceiver at different times, since it is the same continuing material world which is being perceived. According to phenomenalism, however, there is no 'external' world existing independently of perceivers' perceptions of it: there are only perceivers and their perceptions. As Leibniz said, '[a]ccording to this hypothesis, we mean nothing else when we say that Socrates is sitting down than that what we understand by "Socrates" and being "sitting down" is appearing to us and to others' (L 605). According to phenomenalism the 'objective reality' of a public material world consists in the agreement of the subjective perceptions of immaterial minds. In order for perception of a world to be veridical there is no necessity for a perception-independent external world: 'it is enough for the things taking place in one soul to correspond with each other as well as with those happening in any other soul, and it is not necessary to assume anything outside' (L 605).

Leibniz says here that for there to be an objective or inter-subjective reality 'it is enough' for the perceptions of different souls 'to correspond with each other'. In fact, though, not only had he the resources to offer something more than that, but also he probably thought something more was called for. He had to hand *an explanation why* these different perceptions correspond and harmonize, namely that God sees to it that they do. God is 'the only cause of this correspondence between their phenomena' (DM 14). Without the grounding of this divine guarantee his phenomenalistic reduction of a material world to perceptions might well seem like the erection of castles in the air.

One thing phenomenalism has to face is the belief that the world we perceive has features which go beyond what might be being perceived at any one time. Thus the Irish philosopher George Berkeley (1685–1753), with whom the theory in general is usually associated, in speaking of the table on which he was writing, proposed that 'if I were out of my study I should say it existed, meaning thereby that if I was in my study I might perceive it, or that some other spirit actually does perceive it' (Berkeley 1710: 3). In fact Berkeley seems to make two different suggestions here about the table on which he has turned his back. The first is that the table is to be 'reduced' not just to actual perceptions, but also to possible perceptions ('if I was in my study I might perceive it'); the second, 'that some other spirit actually does perceive it', is usually taken to be a reference to omnipresent God. Leibniz, however, had the resources to take 'unperceived' objects in his stride. For him, even without appeal to an omnipresent God, there are (it has been pointed out) no 'gaps in the population's actual experience', no 'unrepresented viewpoints and interrupted conscious histories' (Furth 1967: sect. 3). For Leibniz, the number of perceiving monads is infinite, their perceptions are continuous, and they occupy every possible point of view.

iv. BODY AS MONADIC AGGREGATE

Leibniz's idealism, according to which reality ultimately consists of monads and their perceptions, is sometimes the background of something other than a phenomenalism. Leibniz did not always talk of extended matter as a systematic inter-subjective appearance, an agreement or harmony among the *perceptions* of immaterial monads. Rather differently, he sometimes talked of it as in some way a collection or *aggregate of these perceiving monads* themselves. Thus, calling bodies 'compound substances' he said that they are 'combinations of simple substances or *monads*' (PNG 1).

At first sight there is some continuity here with the account of matter given by his earlier corporeal substance realism. According to that, extended bodies, such as a human corpse or a slab of marble, are composed or aggregated out of smaller corporeal substances. Of course there is discontinuity too. The matter of the earlier view is extended and is aggregated out of smaller and also extended corporeal substances; whereas monads are immaterial and unextended, and the body or composite substance, the result of their aggregation, cannot in any straightforward way be an extended material entity.

A point made by one scholar highlights a difference between Leibniz's phenomenalism and his theory of monadic aggregates (Jolley 1986: 156–7). According to the former, (in which material objects are understood as a systematic appearance or a harmony of monadic perceptions), a given material object does not have any particular set of monads corresponding to it. The harmonized perceptions to which it is 'reduced' are the perceptions of all monads – for each monad perceives the whole world. But according to the theory of monadic aggregates, a given material object is the product of a particular aggregate of monads.

In fact Leibniz did not always say that body is an aggregate *of* monads; he sometimes says that it *results from* them, or that it is a phenomenon *grounded in* them (a '*phenomenon bene fundatum*'). He was, too, sometimes careful to say that monads are not 'parts of' body. 'Properly speaking', he said, 'matter isn't composed of constitutive unities, but results from them, since matter ... is only a phenomenon grounded in things, like a rainbow ... and all reality belongs only to unities. ... Substantial unities [monads] aren't really parts but the foundations of phenomena' (AG 179).

Leibniz's statement that material body, the 'matter of extended mass', is a phenomenon like a rainbow is worth considering. A rainbow is an appearance. It is the way in which in certain circumstances a collection of light-refracting raindrops appears to us. Its properties, such as its colours, are not properties which the rain-drops have; and properties of the raindrops, their chemical composition and their light-refracting propensities, are not properties which the rainbow has. Yet the rainbow is a phenomenon grounded in the raindrops; and the fact that it is an appearance with those properties is to be explained in terms of and as a result of those of the raindrops. In a similar way, Leibniz was suggesting, matter is an appearance, the way in which a collection of monads appears, to other, perceiving monads. Its properties, such as its being extended, are not properties which the monads have, and their properties are not properties which matter has. But, as a phenomenon grounded in the monads, its appearance and its properties are to be explained in terms of, as a result of, those of the monads.

The phenomenon of a rainbow and its properties result from certain light-refracting properties of water drops; similarly, according to Leibniz, the phenomenon of matter and its properties result from certain properties of monads. What are those properties, of matter and of monads, and how do the former result from the latter?

Among the properties of material bodies are sensible qualities such as colour and taste. Along with other advocates of what was called 'the mechanical philosophy' (to be discussed in Chapter 6) Leibniz thought that sensible qualities like these are not 'truly in the nature of external things' (DM 12), but can be explained in terms of the sizes, shapes, and motions of parts of matter. As such, then, they do not result directly from monadic properties, but rather from other properties of material bodies which do have a more direct monadic foundation.

More importantly, therefore, are those properties of material bodies which figure in the mechanical philosophy. As will be explained in detail in Chapter 6, Leibniz identified and discussed in some detail, a number of these. Most obvious is the property of being extended. But this presupposes, he argued, certain other properties, impenetrability and inertia. These constitute what he called the *passive* force of matter. Furthermore, he argued, the phenomenon of motion presupposes that material bodies have *active* force too.

As for the properties of monads which are the foundation of these properties of matter, we will look at these in the next chapter. To anticipate briefly however: monads are characterized by *appetition* and *perception*. The first of these relates to the fact that (as in Chapter 3) they are 'big with their future', and contain a law which details all their future states. 'Appetition' is the active tendency of a monad to move each moment from one of those states to the next. Though Leibniz does not provide anything like detailed explanation of the grounding, it is clear that it is this monadic activity which in some way is the foundation of the active force of phenomenal material body.

A monad's 'perceptions' are the different states through which its appetition takes it. By its perceptions (we saw in Chapter 3), a monad 'mirrors' the whole universe, but not every aspect of what it mirrors is mirrored with the same degree of clarity. Indeed, it is because of this confusion and lack of perceptual clarity that a perceiving monad perceives an aggregate of monads not as an aggregate of monads, but as a phenomenal body. Monadic confusion itself arises from the fact that, as *created* substances, monads are characterized by an element of passivity. Leibniz clearly identifies this monadic passivity as the reality which underlies phenomenal matter's passive force; but, as with active force, there is no real explanation as to how the one gives rise to the other.

FURTHER READING

Broad (1975: ch. 3.5), Garber (1986) are classic accounts of Leibniz as a realist. For Leibniz and phenomenalism see Furth (1967), Jolley (1986), MacDonald Ross (1984), Wilson (1987). For body as aggregated out of monads see Broad (1975: ch. 4.1–4), Rutherford (1995a: 218–26, 1995b: 143–63).

Leibniz's *rejection of atoms*, which figures again in Chapter 5, is addressed in Wilson (1982).

There is an extensive literature on the question as to whether, and if so, just when Leibniz was a *realist*, or an *idealist about corporeal substance*, for example Adams (1994: chs. 9–11), Garber (1996), Hartz (1998), Sleigh (1990a: chs. 5, 6), Wilson (1989: 80–1, 88–110).

MINDS AND MONADS

It is evident from the last two chapters that minds or mind-like entities (forms, entelechies, monads) are of central importance in Leibniz's metaphysical scheme. Whatever objections he had to the Cartesian category of extended substance, he accepted, very broadly speaking, the other Cartesian category, that of thinking substance. In detail, however, there are many important ways in which Leibnizian and Cartesian mind diverge.

i. LEIBNIZIAN AND CARTESIAN MINDS: HUMAN AND ANIMAL

According to the doctrine of hylomorphism, which Leibniz's 'middle period' explanation of 'substance' took up, human beings were not alone in having substantial forms or souls. Non-human animals had them too, as did vegetables and plants. These souls formed a hierarchy, according to the various capacities and abilities of the living things in question. All living things (plant or animal) nourish themselves and reproduce; and these activities were supposed to be governed by a 'vegetative' or 'nutritive' soul. Among living things, animals (human or not) have sense organs, and that required that their soul be 'sensitive' too. Finally, human animals are capable of rational thought and choice, and so were allotted 'rational' or 'intellective' souls. It was a matter of scholastic dispute whether this meant that there was a plurality or (as Leibniz thought) a unity of souls in a human animal.

Descartes thought that this whole schema of forms was mistaken. He construed all 'living' things, other than humans (and higher beings such as angels) in purely material terms. He held that all the functions which the scholastics referred to 'sensitive' or

'vegetative' souls were to be understood solely in terms of physical mechanisms. Everything from the digestion of food, through to
the reception of stimuli by the eyes and ears and the movements of
the limbs in appropriate reaction were, for him, all to be explained
mechanically. All the functions of non-human animals 'follow from
the mere arrangement' of its organs, he said. This takes place 'every
bit as naturally as the movements of a clock or other automaton
follow from the arrangement of its counter-weights and wheels'
(CSM 1.108).

In respect of the functions which were formerly attributed to
'vegetative' or 'sensitive' souls, humans were no different from other
animals, for Descartes. Any of the activities human animals had in
common with other creatures were to be understood mechanically.
But, as animals capable of understanding and rational thought,
humans had been supposed to have 'intellective' souls also. Unlike
some of his materialist contemporaries, such as Hobbes, Descartes
did not seek to absorb the functions of this kind of form into the
mechanical workings of material substance. He assigned them to
an immaterial mind, the unique possession of human beings (and
angels). However, having observed that animals do not appear to
have the kind of mental life that humans do, Descartes concluded
that they have no mental life at all, and that there are 'no souls in
animals' (PNG 4).

Leibniz continued to recognize something like the traditional
distinctions between different kinds of 'soul' or 'substantial form'.
In disagreement with Descartes and his followers he recognizes
different kinds of soul, with different levels of mental activity.
For Leibniz non-human animals were something more than mere
machines; for him there *are* 'souls in animals', animals do have some
kind of 'mental' life.

Humans alone, however, were supposed capable of *thought*
and *understanding*. They are characterized by possession of a '*mind*'
or '*spirit*', Leibniz's terms for a *rational* soul specifically. Part of
what Leibniz is thinking of here in distinguishing human from non-
human animals is that humans are capable of the sort of reasoning
involved in logic, mathematics, and geometry, and can come to a
scientific understanding of the world.

According to the *Monadology*, '[o]ur reasonings are founded on
two great principles' (Mon 31): the principle of sufficient reason and
the principle of contradiction. According to the first, 'there can be

no real or existing fact, no true statement, unless there is a sufficient reason, why it should be so and not otherwise, although these reasons usually cannot be known by us' (Mon 32); according to the second, anything that involves a contradiction is false and its opposite is true. Leibniz associated these principles with a distinction between two kinds of truth, a distinction which his contemporaries would have recognized and which is still common philosophical currency. On the one hand are *contingent* truths of fact, whose opposite is not impossible (examples might be that ice is cold to the touch, or that Alexander the Great died from poison). We know their truth on the basis of experience or history. On the other hand are *necessary* truths, whose opposites are impossible and involve a contradiction (examples might be that $4 \times 112 = 448$, or that bachelors are unmarried). They can be proved by pure reasoning, independently of experience, 'by analysis … into simpler ideas and truths' (Mon 33). Just as we might, Leibniz spoke of their necessity as 'logical', but he also characterized it as 'metaphysical', and having in mind that necessary truths must always be true, and that their truth can be shown by the analysis of ideas, or essences (or 'concepts' we might say), he sometimes referred to them as 'eternal' or 'essential' truths.

The reasoning associated with the principle of contradiction was called 'demonstrative'. It begins with those 'necessary or eternal' truths, for example that the angles of a triangle sum to two right-angles. From these it moves by 'infallible' steps to 'indubitable' conclusions (as that the external angle of a triangle is equal to the sum of its two internal opposites) (PNG 5). The possibility that space might be non-Euclidian had not yet been entertained and 'eternal' truths were conceived to be truths which would hold in any world that God might have created. Accordingly, Leibniz speaks of them as comprising the sciences which deal with the necessary structure of the world. They have to do with the way in which God was bound to have created and 'ordered things (by weight, measure, number, etc.)'.

The thought that humans can be mathematicians and geometers and can come to a rational understanding of the ways in which God 'ordered things' in the world is very important to Leibniz. As we will see again in Chapter 10, it means, in effect, that humans are able to trace or reproduce in their minds what God himself has done; they are able, he says, to 'imitate', on a smaller scale, 'what God performs in the great world' (PNG 14). Leibniz sees this as a way in which humans enter into 'a kind of society' with God (PNG 15).

Being capable of the kind of abstract thought required for the knowledge and understanding of the necessary truths of the sciences links us to God in another way too. For from this kind of thought we progress to acts of reflection by which rational souls become self-aware. Rational souls can think of 'what is called *I*, and consider that this or that is within us' (Mon 30). This reflection on itself leads a rational soul to think metaphysically. It leads it to think about 'being', 'substance', and immaterial things. And these thoughts, when carried through, bring us to realize that while we are limited God is unlimited.

The awareness we rational souls have of ourselves is not merely of the moment. We are aware of ourselves as persisting through time: we have memory and can look to the future. Unlike non-human animals we are aware of ourselves as having a history, of what has happened to us and of what we have done. This awareness gives us a moral dimension. It means, for example, that we are susceptible of punishment and reward. Without the memory of the past, those things would not mean anything to us and we could not benefit from them.

The 'thinking' which was the essential feature of Cartesian mind was somewhat broader than the 'rational understanding' which characterizes a Leibnizian rational soul or mind. Descartes intended that 'willing, understanding, imagining, sensing and so on are just different ways of thinking, and all belong to the soul' (K 32). So some things which previously had been assigned to the 'sensitive soul', such as sensing, were the province of Cartesian mind. This meant that according to Descartes, non-human animals, which lacked a soul or mind of any kind, did not, in all strictness, sense. Perception was not for him an awareness, common to us and the brute animals, of a physical environment. It was simply a movement in the material brain, common to us and the brutes, but which, for us, was accompanied with sensations or thoughts in an immaterial mind.

Leibniz, however, followed the scholastics, in holding that while non-human animals differed from humans in lacking a rational soul, they were all alike in having a 'sensitive soul'. Distinguishing them from 'rational souls' or 'minds', Leibniz calls them simply 'souls'. The characteristic of all animals, whether human or non-human, is the activity of sensation. 'Sensation' is made possible by the fact that animal bodies have sense organs, such as eyes and ears. These focus, or make distinct, the impressions made on the body by sound-waves, light-rays and so on.

Though unlike Descartes Leibniz did not think they are mere machines, non-human animals (for which he uses the traditional term 'brute') are not capable of thought and understanding. They are, though, capable of something which, in a certain way, is like thought. 'There is', he says 'a connexion between the perceptions of animals, which has some resemblance to reason' (PNG 5). When a dog runs away from someone with a stick with which it is used to being beaten, there is no reasoning of the kind which might be represented deductively: 'so far this person has beaten me with a stick; the future will be like the past; therefore he is going to beat me now and I must run away'. The dog runs away simply because, as Leibniz says, 'memory represents to him the pain which was caused by that stick'. As he puts it, the dog is acting 'empirically', rather than 'rationally' (PNG 5).

Interestingly, Leibniz anticipates here some of the ideas on empirical knowledge usually associated with the Scottish philosopher David Hume (1711–1776). He observes that in the normal course of things we human beings, though capable of rational thought, often act just like animals. We are 'empirical' in three quarters of what we do. We act on the basis of association of ideas. We expect the sun to rise tomorrow simply 'because we have always experienced it to be so' (PNG 5). Only an astronomer is able to make a rational prediction, not on the basis merely of the past *facts* of the sun's always having risen, but on the basis of his knowledge of the *causes* of its having done so.

But even this is not to say, Leibniz recognized, that the astronomer's reasoning is as fully rational as that of a mathematician or a geometer. The reasoning in both cases is *deductive* in that its steps are logical, but the astronomer's reasoning is not properly *demonstrative*. Its premises are not truths which are necessarily and eternally true. Rather it is based on what Leibniz called 'truths of fact', contingent truths whose opposite is possible, facts about the daily rotation of the earth on its axis. These facts could have been different, and indeed might change, he says. Exactly how, why and when he has in mind is not clear, but Leibniz evidently believes that they will change. The astronomer's prediction, he comments, 'will ultimately fail when the cause of daylight, which is not eternal, ceases' (PNG 5).

It is, then, a feature of human beings, with their rational souls, that they are capable of an awareness of themselves, an ability to say 'I'. This self-awareness, for Leibniz, is not shared by 'brutes', such as horses and dogs. This does not mean that non-human animals have no stream of perceptions running through their soul. Their lack of self-reflection does not mean they do not feel pain, though it does mean they do not experience the more sophisticated feelings of joy and grief.

Descartes' definition of 'thought', the essential feature of the immaterial mind, effectively denies this distinction which Leibniz recognized between sensations and other mental occurrences on the one hand, and a reflexive awareness of them on the other. He defines 'thought' as 'everything which we are aware of as happening within us, in so far as we have awareness of it' (CSM 1.195). Thoughts 'happen within us', in our minds, and we are aware of their doing so; but it is only *in so far as we are aware of them* that they are thoughts for Descartes. All mental activity for Descartes was *self-aware*.

According to Leibniz it was just this running together of thought as awareness and the reflexive awareness of thought, which lay behind Descartes' rather startling view that dogs and cats are as insensate as clocks. It is not merely according to Descartes, that non-human animals do not engage in rational thought: it is also that they do not feel, perceive or sense. Unlike clocks, they are natural machines and not the product of human artifice; but there the difference ends. According to Leibniz however, it was because they disregarded perceptions which are not perceived that the Cartesians were led to believe that animals have no souls.

Arnauld too objected to Descartes that surely it is possible for there to be 'many things in our minds of which the mind is not aware' (CSM 2.150). But Descartes was not alone in not recognizing the possibility of the kind of self-unaware mental life that Leibniz attributed to non-human animals. Locke agreed with him, holding that nothing thinks '*without being conscious of it*, or perceiving, that it does so' (Locke 1690: 2.1.19). However, some comments on Locke made by another seventeenth-century philosopher, Thomas Sergeant, bring out nicely the Cartesian mistake of running together two different things in saying that thought or any mental activity is not possible without simultaneous awareness of it. He reminds us how

> when a man is quite absorbed in a serious thought, or (as we say) in a brown study, his mind is so totally taken up with the object of his present contemplation ... that he can have no thought, at that very instant, of his own internal operation, or that he is thinking, or any thing like it (Sergeant 1697: 121–2).

But this does not mean that the man is *not* thinking!

Of course it is true that we *are* often aware of our awareness; we may, for example, be listening to music with, as we say, half a mind and aware of ourselves as doing so with the other half. It is also true that even though we can be 'quite absorbed' by something, we always emerge from our 'brown study' and 'come to ourselves'. But the kind of non-reflexive awareness which Sergeant suggests we are sometimes capable of is just the kind of awareness Leibniz characterizes animals as always having, of their bodily pains and, via their sense organs, of their environment.

So though we human beings are capable of reflexive awareness of what is going on in our minds we are not always aware of our perceptions. Indeed, Leibniz said, it is and must be the case that perceiving is continual and that there are perceptions of which we are not aware. '[A]t every moment', he said, 'there is in us an infinity of perceptions, unaccompanied by awareness or reflection' (NE 53). These confused, unconscious perceptions do have an effect on our mental state as a whole, moreover. Leibniz illustrated this with the sound of the sea. In hearing this noise, he argued, we must hear its parts, the noise of each wave. The noise of the sea is a confused one, made up of faint 'minute perceptions' of each wave, which we do not hear separately (NE 54). The plain fact of human life that we have shifts of attention, degrees of concentration, can faint or fall asleep, is a further illustration of the idea that there are degrees of confusion and awareness among perceptions. We do not always 'pay heed to certain of our own present perceptions, we allow them to slip by unconsidered and even unnoticed' (NE 54). When someone alerts us to a noise we may realize that we had been aware of it, but had not at the time been aware that we had been.

Moreover, we are never so soundly asleep that we do not have 'some feeble and confused sensations' (NE 54). This must be the case, for unless we had some dim awareness of its beginning, even the loudest noise could not awake us. We will see in Chapter 8 that an important case of a rational soul having unconscious perceptions is after what we call 'death', which, he said, 'can only be a sleep' (NE 55).

ii. MONADIC PERCEPTION, APPETITION, AND EMBODIMENT

Rational souls (or minds, spirits), and brute or animal souls all come under the more general classification of 'entelechy' or 'monad'.

In addition to them Leibniz's scheme includes yet a third type of 'entelechy' – 'bare monads'. These characterize even more basic living things. The difference for Aristotle between living things in general and inanimate matter was the fact of self-nutrition. For Leibniz, however, the principle of life was *perception* (and the mental activity he called 'appetition'). The difference between perception, which is a feature of any living thing even the most primitive, and *sensation*, is that the latter is 'focussed' or 'heightened' perception, which involves the possession of sense organs. It might seem more natural to us to have used 'perception' more restrictively, in connection with sophisticated sense organs such as the eyes, and not to cover any reaction to light, such as the heliotropic movement of some plants. But, in Leibniz's technical use of the term, 'perception' is the basic activity of monads of all three types, and 'sensation' or heightened perception is explained in terms of it. Moreover, not only is sensation, the conscious activity of the animal 'soul', explained in terms of perception, but the self-aware perception, or 'apperception', of 'minds' or 'spirits', is explained in its terms too. It is defined as 'reflective knowledge' or awareness of the inner state of perception (PNG 4). Perception in bare primitive monads is utterly unconscious, and Leibniz thinks of them as existing always in a state of dull stupor like ours when we are asleep or in a faint.

The elements of the perceptual states of bare monads will never be other than confused and unclear. But even the states of the two higher types of monad, which are capable of heightened focussed perception, will not always be clear and differentiated. If it is true that monadic perception contains some representation of the past and the future, and mirrors the whole of the world, it clearly must have unconscious elements. We are obviously not consciously aware of a large part of the infinite complexity of such omni-perception. When we are looking at a vase of flowers on the table, we are not aware of the bustle of market day in a distant town. The fact that a monad's perceptions are of different degrees of distinctness in this way is, in effect, the same as the fact that 'each monad mirrors the whole universe *from its own special point of view*'. Although a monad is not restricted to representing 'only a part of things' this 'representation is only confused as regards the detail of the entire universe, and can be distinct as regards a small part of things, namely, those which are either nearest or greatest in relation to each of the monads' (Mon 60).

Though it often occurs as 'apperception' in rational minds, and as 'sensation' in animal souls, 'perception' is a fundamental characteristic of all monads, of whatever grade, even the lowest. A state of perception is defined as something which 'involves and represents a multitude in the unity' (Mon 14). The 'unity' in which the 'multitude' is represented is, of course, the perceiving monad itself. As for the 'multitude', it is a function partly of the fact that a monad's present state of perception contains elements which relate to all its past and future states, and partly also of the fact that a monad is a mirror, not merely of its immediate environment, but of the whole world. So the perceptual state of a monad at any time consists not only of elements relating to its past and future, but also of elements which correspond to the perceptual states (past, present and future) of an infinite number of other monads.

The confusion there is in perception arises from a kind of passivity, and this monadic passivity underlies and accounts for some of the properties of the phenomenon of material body, the appearance which an aggregate of monads presents to other monadic perceivers (as we saw at the end of the last chapter). Specifically, these properties are extension and, more basically, impenetrability and inertia.

Perception is not the only fundamental feature of monads. Their perceptual states are transitory and change at every moment in accordance with 'a detailed specification' of its future which the monad contains – a specification which during Leibniz's middle years was associated with complete concepts and substantial forms. One feature of these changes is (as we saw in Chapter 3) that their cause is purely internal, and this 'action of the internal principle that produces the change or passage from one perception to another' (Mon 15) is a second fundamental monadic feature. Leibniz names it 'appetition'. This active element in monads underlies a further important property of the 'well-founded phenomenon' of material body, an 'active force' connected with motion. Just how the 'active force' of body is grounded in monadic appetition Leibniz does not make clear.

Inasmuch as monadic perceptual states differ accordingly as they consist of more, or less, distinct, developed, unconfused perceptions, they differ in their degree of 'perfection'. The soul, Leibniz said, 'has perfection in proportion to its distinct perceptions' (PNG 13). Given this, it follows that a monad may move on from a less to a more perfect state, or from a more to a less perfect state, and it is in terms of this that Leibniz introduced the idea of a monad's being either active or passive:

> [I]f we take 'action' to be an endeavour towards perfection, and 'passion' [i.e. passivity] to be the opposite, then genuine substances are active only when their perceptions ... are becoming better developed and more distinct, just as they are passive only when their perceptions are becoming more confused. (NE 210)

Since monads 'mirror the whole world' their perceptions are often representations of the states of other monads, and Leibniz thought of monadic actions and passions as being reciprocal. Despite the fact that monads do not interact they may be related in that an action in one can correspond to a passion in another. So the one monad can be said to have acted on the other, and the changes in the one explain or give a reason for the changes in the other. 'The action of one finite substance on another consists solely in the increase in the degree of its expression together with the diminution of that of the other, in so far as God has made them conform to each other' (DM 15).

As we saw in Chapter 2, monads, of whatever kind, are never disembodied. Every monad is the 'soul' of a corporeal substance. Leibniz held quite firmly that 'every Spirit, every soul ... is always united with a body and ... no soul is ever entirely without one' (NE 58). It is because it is associated with a body that a monad mirrors, represents or perceives the whole universe. For as its body is part of the causally connected plenum of the material world, so through its association with its body a monad perceives that whole world. Like Descartes before him, Leibniz rejected the idea that there is any empty space, and so the slightest movement in a body 'has an effect on adjacent bodies and thereby on further bodies and so on *ad infinitum*, but proportionately decreased' (LA 112). Thus, as a monad's body 'expresses the whole universe through the connection of all matter in the plenum', so the soul also mirrors and represents the whole universe 'by representing this body, which belongs to it in a particular way' (Mon 62).

According to one of Leibniz's accounts of it, material body is an aggregate of monads. On this account, a monad's *own body*, will, just as any other material thing, be nothing but an aggregate of other monads. But it will of course be one to which it bears a special relation, a relation different from that which it bears to other things in the universe. Leibniz said that 'the body which is specially assigned to it, and of which it is the entelechy' (Mon 62) is what a monad perceives more distinctly than any other thing. So given that he also said that nearer objects are perceived more distinctly than more distant ones, we might be led to suppose that a monad's body is simply that material object which it perceives as being nearest to it. But this is hardly satisfactory since it is only in virtue of having a body that a monad can be said to have a spatial position in the first place. Moreover, some of our perceptions of someone else's hand could be as distinct as those of our own. But their hand still does not belong to us as ours does; I can perceive it in ways I cannot perceive theirs. Nearness or distinctness, as such, does not capture what it is to have a body, what it is to be embodied.

Leibniz also said, however, that the monad which is the mind of a corporeal substance (the substance's 'central' (PNG 3) monad) 'dominates' the monads which constitute, or present the appearance of, its material body. Perhaps the idea here is that what makes my hand mine, and part of my body, is that I can 'dominate' it, move it in a way in which I can't move someone else's. Another way of putting this would be to say that I am, or can be, active with respect to my hand; and, as we have seen above, 'activity' is something which Leibniz explains, not so much in terms of the degree of distinctness of a perceptual state, but rather in terms of *an increase* in that degree of distinctness as a monad moves from one perceptual state to another. Yet though I can be active with respect to my hand, I can of course also be passive. When the skin of my hand is punctured with a pin, then, in Leibniz's terms, I move to a lower degree of perfection and feel pain. So it is not always true that the monad which is the mind of a corporeal substance 'dominates' those which constitute its body; rather there is a reciprocity of 'domination'.

There seems to be a further element in Leibniz's account of the relation between the 'central' monad and those which constitute its body. This resonates with the idea that a monad represents its body 'more distinctly' than it does the rest of the universe, and that its perceptions correspond 'particularly' to its body. It also resonates with there being a 'reciprocity of domination' between mind and body. This is Leibniz's suggestion that there is a certain 'directness' of expression or representation between them, an 'agreement' which is something more than or different from the fact that all monads perceive or represent all others. What the soul *primarily* expresses is its body, for it is *through it*, as part of the material plenum, that it expresses and mirrors the rest of the universe. '[T]he nature of the soul is to represent the body' (AG 173). The body is similarly an expression of the mind. As one scholar has put it:

> Every monad expresses everything in the whole universe ... but each monad expresses, and is expressed by, its own organic body in a special way. ... A monad and its organic body both *contain* expressions of an infinity of things, but each *is*, as a whole, an expression of the other, and this relationship of mutual expression is peculiarly direct. (Adams 1994: 286)

This idea of expression is discussed further in Chapter 8.

It is plain from all of this that Leibniz relies rather heavily on the idea of degrees of confusedness, and clarity or distinctness in monadic perception. He uses it to differentiate between the different grades of monad; he links it to consciousness; he invokes it in connection with the idea of 'minute perceptions', such as make up the confused noise of the sea; he appeals to it in explaining how monads have a 'point of view' or perspective on the world; and it figures in his account of the nature of the relation between mind and body. He also uses 'clarity of perception' to explain the difference between sensation and the rational thought of which the highest grade of monads, spirits or minds, are capable: 'distinct knowledge ... occurs in the actual use of reason; but the senses supply us with confused thoughts' (T 303). It is easy to understand that commentators have felt that it is too one-dimensional and unexplained to serve all these purposes with ease.

FURTHER READING

For discussion of the different grades of mind and their perceptions see Brandom (1981), Kulstad (1983), McRae (1976: ch. 3), Parkinson (1982); for rationality as distinct perception see Alles (1933), McRae (1976: ch. 4), Parkinson (1982).

For a discussion of relative distinctness and point of view see Adams (1994: 251–3, 285–91), Broad (1975: ch. 4.3), Furth (1967: 16–22), Rutherford (1995b: 149–53).

CHAPTER 6

NATURAL PHILOSOPHY

i. THE MECHANICAL PHILOSOPHY AND SUBSTANTIAL FORMS

The seventeenth century was one of huge advances in scientific knowledge. It saw the publication of, for example, Kepler's *New Astronomy* (1609), Harvey's *Essay on the Motion of the Heart and Blood* (1628), Galileo's *Dialogues on the Two Chief Systems of the World* (1632) and, most spectacularly, Newton's *Mathematical Principles of Natural Philosophy* (1687). The thinking behind much of the detailed theoretical and experimental scientific work done then embodied a general picture of how the material world 'worked' and was 'structured'. The picture was given by the so-called 'mechanical philosophy'. Though the mechanical philosophy flourished in the seventeenth century its ideas were not new, and can be found in the classical atomic theory of the early Greek philosophers Democritus (c. 460–c. 370 B.C.), and Epicurus (341–270 B.C.). According to them, the properties of material things are to be explained by reference to the atoms which were supposed to make them up. The world was supposed to consist of no more than these material atoms, and the collisions between them, as they moved through the void of space, were what underlay all the familiar phenomena and events of the world.

Many of the mechanical philosophers of the seventeenth century (e.g. Descartes and Leibniz) were not atomists and did not think that matter consisted of ultimate and indivisible particles, but like the earlier philosophers they supposed that the properties of material things are to be explained by reference to the actions and reactions on and with each other of their constituent parts. This mechanical, 'matter and motion', picture of the world contrasted with the 'hylomorphic picture' which derived from scholastic metaphysics. According to this, as we saw in Chapter 3, the material world consists of substances, each with its own essence, nature or substantial form, which explains and makes intelligible its properties and behaviour. Thus the doctrine that the characteristic activities of living things (humans, animals, plants) are to be attributed to their substantial forms or souls, was extended to the inanimate world, and the proponents of the 'new mechanical philosophy' rejected it firmly.

Robert Boyle was one of the 'new philosophers' who criticized the scholastic doctrine and argued for the mechanical philosophy according to which the material world is nothing but matter in motion. '[A]lmost all sorts of qualities, most of which have been by the Schools left unexplicated, or generally referred to I know not what incomprehensible forms, *may* be produced mechanically', he said (Boyle 1666: 17). The scientist or 'naturalist'

> in explicating *particular phenomena* considers only the *size, shape, motion* (or *want of it*), *texture*, and the resulting qualities and attributes, of the small particles of matter. And thus in this great *automaton*, the world (as in a watch or a clock) ... the phenomena it exhibits are to be accounted for by the *number, bigness, proportion, shape, motion* (or *endeavour*), *rest*, ... of the ... parts it is made up of. (Boyle 1666: 71)

Descartes was one of the first of the early modern philosophers to reject substantial forms and to favour the 'mechanical philosophy'. He laid it down in his *Principles of Philosophy* (1644) that all natural phenomena are ultimately to be explained in terms of 'the shape, size, position and motion of particles of matter' (CSM 1.279). This is 'much better', he said, 'than explaining matters by inventing all sorts of strange objects ... [such as] "substantial forms" ... which are harder to understand than the things they are supposed to explain' (CSM 1.287).

Leibniz too was a committed advocate of the 'matter in motion' world picture. He firmly rejected any idea that explanations in the natural sciences might be in terms of substantial forms. He was absolutely clear that reference to such forms has no place 'in the details of physics, and should not be used for explaining the particulars of phenomena' (DM 10). He was equally convinced that natural phenomena 'can be explained mathematically or mechanically' (DM 18). '[I]n explaining corporeal phenomena, we must not unnecessarily resort to ... any ... form ... [E]verything should be derived from the nature of body ... magnitude, figure, and motion' (L 110). The scholastics thought they could explain the properties of bodies simply by referring to forms, 'without taking the trouble to examine their manner of operation'. It was as if one said that a clock's form gave it a time-indicative quality 'without considering what that consists in' (DM 10).

Given the use he makes of substantial forms in his 'realist' account of corporeal substance (as in Chapter 3) one might wonder how Leibniz could be such an advocate of the 'mechanical philosophy', which rejects those very substantial forms. There is no inconsistency here, however. What he denies is that substantial forms have any place in *physics*, in detailed explanations of natural phenomena. What he insists on is that they are essential for an adequate *metaphysical* account of the world. It is, moreover, of vital importance in understanding his ideas to appreciate that there is no disconnection in his thinking either. It is not that he held something in one context which he denied in another. On the contrary, there are close parallels and connections between the detail of his thinking about physics (in which substantial forms are rejected) and his metaphysics of corporeal substance (in which forms have an important role). It is a fundamental of his philosophy of science that without an adequate metaphysics (which will involve appeal to substantial forms), physics will lack proper foundation. '[A]lthough all the particular phenomena of [corporeal] nature can be explained mathematically or mechanically ... nevertheless ... the general principles of corporeal mechanical nature itself are metaphysical ... belonging to forms or indivisible natures' (DM 18). In other words, we can understand everything matter *does* with no reference to substantial forms, but to understand what matter *is* they are crucial.

ii. MATTER AND PASSIVE FORCE

According to the mechanical philosophy, then, the material world is, at bottom, a world of matter in motion. We saw in Chapter 3 how Leibniz disagrees with Descartes about the metaphysical status of this matter. For Descartes it is, in and of itself, substantial, for it is spatially extended and so possessed of one of two principal attributes which constitute a substantial essence. Leibniz, however, did not accept extension as a substantial essence, did not accept that matter or body considered simply as extended was substantial.

Now besides disagreeing with Descartes about corporeal substance and the metaphysical status of body or matter, Leibniz also disagreed with him about what the mechanical philosophy required of matter as to its physical properties. There was no doubt that extension is *an* important feature of it; he was at one with Descartes in holding that 'only what is thought of as extended can be called a body' (L 143). But it was a serious error to think that it is *the* 'principal attribute' of body. To begin with (as we shall see in detail), it does not give rise to all the properties with which the physical science of bodies needs to deal: 'neither motion or action nor resistance or passion can be derived from it. As a consequence, the natural laws which are observed in the motion and collision of bodies arise from the concept of extension alone' (L 390). Finally (and again we shall see this in detail), it is not as basic as Descartes thought.

Leibniz was not alone in thinking that there was something missing from matter as Descartes conceived it. Other adherents to the mechanical philosophy felt it was too thin, as it were. It lacked substance, so to speak. What was most often felt to be missing from it was 'impenetrability', the property in virtue of which no two bodies can occupy the same space, and so the property by virtue of which one body colliding with another will displace it. In partial defence of Descartes it must be pointed out that his doctrine that the nature of body consists solely in extension does not entail that there are no other properties which characterize it. Descartes certainly thought that there were, and impenetrability was a case in point. In fact they were a *consequence* of extension. He explained to the English philosopher Henry More who corresponded with him about it, that saying that body is essentially just extension does not mean that it is not necessarily impenetrable too. While not of the essence of body, impenetrability, he said, 'belongs to the essence of extension'. His idea, it seems, was that in being extended body is thereby impenetrable. 'It is impossible to conceive of one part of extended substance penetrating another equal part without *eo ipso* thinking that half the total extension is taken away or annihilated' (K 249).

In thinking that impenetrability automatically follows from extension, Descartes was effectively following some medieval philosophers. But in Leibniz's view this got things quite the wrong way around. It is not that matter is impenetrable and excludes other bodies because it is extended and fills space. It is, rather, that it is extended and fills space, because it is impenetrable.

In coming to this conclusion Leibniz began by reflecting that Descartes was wrong to think of extension as a basic property. Body cannot merely be extended and fill space. There must be something *prior to* extension, some other quality *in virtue of which* it is extended and fills space. Extension must be relative to something more basic than it. Extension must presuppose something more fundamental. It implies 'some quality, some attribute, some nature in this subject, which is extended, is expanded with the subject, and is continued. Extension is the diffusion of that quality or nature' (AG 261). Leibniz uses the 'extension or diffusion' of qualities such as whiteness through milk, or hardness through a diamond, in illustration of this idea that there must be some property diffused through an extended thing in virtue of which it is extended and which, so to speak, 'gives it body'.

The property which Leibniz concludes constitutes 'materiality' (AG 622) and which, as he says, is the 'essence of matter or the form itself of corporeity' (La 637) is impenetrability or solidity. This is the property which underlies the fact that 'a body does not give place to another body ... unless it can move elsewhere' (L 392). (He sometimes refers to it as 'antitipy'.) He thought that the reason why Descartes had mistakenly eliminated it as part of the nature of body was that he confused it with the quite different property of hardness. Hardness is not an essential property of body; not all bodies are hard. A hard body will not yield its shape under pressure; a soft one will. Solidity or impenetrability, however, is an essential property; all bodies are solid. It is what makes it impossible for two bodies, hard or soft, to occupy the same place.

A properly worked out mechanical philosophy needs fully to recognize solidity or impenetrability, Leibniz argued. For unless bodies were mutually impenetrable they would not displace each other in the collisions which, according to that philosophy, are the basis of natural phenomena. They would not have what Leibniz called 'mobility'; unless they were solid, 'a body could not be pushed or moved by another body' (AG 261–2). In arguing for the recognition of solidity or impenetrability Leibniz was in agreement not only with, as we have seen, Locke, and More, but also with Boyle and Newton. However, with the possible exception of Newton, he went further than them and insisted on yet a further property.

The mechanical philosophers naturally supposed that what happens to the motions of material bodies after they have collided is not arbitrary, but law-governed and regular. People such as Descartes, Gassendi, Huygens and Malebranche devoted much intellectual effort to trying to discover and formulate the laws of motion. According to Descartes they, at least the more general ones, could be deduced from the nature of God. According to Malebranche they were the result of God's voluntary choice. Leibniz, however, held that they must flow from the nature of matter itself. This of course meant, arguing backwards, that the nature of matter must be suited for the law-like regularities which we can discover matter is subject to.

Leibniz held, accordingly, that if matter were nothing more than solid extension then the laws of nature would be other than we in fact observe them to be. It must therefore have some further property. Besides being solid and extended it must also have the property of what he called 'inertia'. 'From this', he said, 'follow laws of motion far different than they would be if only impenetrability and extension were in bodies and their matter' (NI 11).

He reasoned in this way. Solidity means that two bodies cannot occupy the same space. It follows that one solid body cannot come to occupy the place of another unless it moves that other body out of the way. But solidity gives no reason why a small moving body which collides with a large and stationary body might not just move it along with it, with undiminished speed. It gives no reason why any number of other results might not obtain. It gives no reason why the size of the colliding bodies is relevant. It places no constraints on the results of a collision between them, except that they cannot end up occupying the same place. The world would be chaotic, Leibniz argues, if it were 'no more difficult to put a large body into motion than a small one' (AG 124).

We have to recognize, therefore, not just that a stationary body is impenetrable by another. We must also see that 'matter resists being moved through a certain *natural inertia*' (NI 11). In order to get a stationary body to move this inertia needs to be overcome by, and at some cost to the motion of, the colliding body: matter 'is not indifferent to motion and rest ... but requires more active force for motion in proportion to its size' (NI 11).

By the 'size' of a body, to which its 'inertia' is proportional, Leibniz does not mean its bulk or volume. He has in mind in effect what Newton in his *Principles* called its 'mass'; and it is clearly something which Descartes (for whom the amount of matter of a body is simply its volume) is not well placed to recognize.

Leibniz calls the two properties of extended material body, 'impenetrability', and 'inertia', its 'passive force of resistance' or 'passive power'. As we saw in Chapter 4, according to his idealist account of material body, matter is a well-founded phenomenon (analogous to a rainbow). As such, its properties such as its extend-edness and impenetrability are derived from those of the aggregated monads which present the phenomenal appearance of matter. Thus, extension, so Leibniz had argued, is not a primitive property but presupposes something which is 'diffused', 'continued' or 'repeated'. At the monadic level what is repeated, by the aggregated monads, is the monadic nature itself, and one feature of this nature is a kind of passivity. It is this monadic passivity which (in a way which Leibniz leaves rather unexplained) is the metaphysical reality underlying the 'passive force' of phenomenal extended matter, its 'impenetrability' and 'inertia'.

But extended matter considered as it has these properties is still no more than an incomplete abstraction for Leibniz. A complete account of the matter of the world of the mechanical philosophy, the matter which makes up marble tiles, or colliding billiard balls, requires the recognition of a further very important property. This feature of matter has its ultimate foundation in and is an 'echo' of the primary active force which characterizes monadic appetition. We should now look in detail at this 'derived' force, which Leibniz calls 'active force'.

iii. MOTION AND ACTIVE FORCE

Along with matter, motion is one of the two components of the physical world according to the mechanical philosophy. Much of Leibniz's thinking about it took place, as with so much of his philosophy, against the background of Descartes' contributions to the subject.

Descartes pointed out that while a man sitting in the stern of a ship 'remains in one place relative to the other parts of the ship ... he is constantly changing his place relative to the neighbouring shores'

(CSM 1.228). Leibniz agreed with this as an initial thought: considered kinematically, or 'geometrically', purely as it appears, motion 'consists in a mere relation' (La 685). Given a pair of bodies moving relatively to each other, we cannot tell from the appearances alone which one (or both) is really moving. Leibniz then argued that there must be some underlying 'causes' (La 685). There must be some dynamical reality beneath the merely kinematical appearances. For something to be moving it is necessary 'not only that it change its position with respect to other things but also that there be within itself a cause of change, a force, an action' (L 393).

Leibniz had another argument for the conclusion that there must be a dynamical force underlying motion. When it moves from one place to another, a body occupies intermediate places at intermediate times: motion, that is, takes place over a period of time. Now, Leibniz argued, 'a whole never exists, inasmuch as it lacks coexisting parts'. So if motion is understood purely kinematically, simply as an object being in one place at one moment and in another at the next, it 'strictly speaking ... never really exists' (AG 118): it has parts which never exist together. Consequently, if there is any reality in motion, there must be something true of a moving body *at each moment* of its movement. Again, at any moment, there is, to all appearances, no difference between a stationary body and a moving one. But there *must* be some difference *at that moment* between the two bodies, for one is a moving body and the other is not. The moving body must, Leibniz concludes, possess a moving force. '[A]s for *motion*, that which is real in it is *force* or power; that is to say, what there is in the present state which carries with it a change in the future. The rest is only phenomena and relations' (WF 85). Leibniz sometimes calls this 'motive force' *vis viva*, or 'living force'.

This idea that there is something in the present state of a moving body which carries with it a change for the future has obvious resonating parallels with other parts of Leibniz's thought which we have encountered earlier. It echoes his metaphysical doctrines (as in Chapters 3 and 5) to the effect that substances are 'big with their future', and that monads have 'appetition', an active tendency to move on from one state to another.

Though Leibniz made much more of it, his idea that a moving body has a force associated with it is one which he shares with Descartes. But it has a far longer history than that. To understand it properly we should look at its roots. These, as so often in the history of philosophy, lie in Aristotle.

Aristotle reasoned that a moving thing must be being moved by something: there must be a 'motor' by which it is, so to speak, 'carried along'. The source of its motion can be 'internal' to it (as in what Aristotle called 'natural' motion) or can be 'external' (as in 'unnatural' or 'violent' motion). The motion of a thrown javelin is 'unnatural'; if the javelin had been 'left to itself' and simply let loose from a stationary hand, its 'natural' movement would have been downwards. So, in its lateral movement through the air, a thrown javelin must have a continuous 'external' source of motion.

One theory discussed by Aristotle was the theory of 'antiperistasis'. According to this, the javelin in its lateral motion is being continuously pushed along by air which comes round from its front end to its rear. Another theory, also discussed by Aristotle, was that the throwing hand, as it releases the javelin, passes on to the air its ability to act as a 'motor'; and this ability is then communicated from one parcel of air to another. So, as though moving by being passed from hand to hand, the javelin moves by being successively passed to different parcels of air. A third idea was suggested in the sixth century by Philoponous. According to this, it is the javelin itself, not the air through which it passes, which gets from the throwing hand a motive force which continuously sustains its motion.

This last idea was at the heart of the so-called *impetus theory of motion*. According to one of its foremost proponents in the fourteenth century, John Buridan, there is 'impressed' in a moving projectile

> something which is [its] motive force ... [T]he motor [i.e. the source of motion] in moving a moving body impresses in it a certain impetus or a certain moving force ... It is by that impetus that the stone is moved after the projector ceases to move. (Quoted Clagett 1959: 523)

The thought that associated with a body's motion there is a sustaining force, an impetus, can be found in Descartes. He refers to a moving body's 'force of motion' (CSM 1.95) or 'power of persisting in its motion' (CSM 1.244). But he does not dwell on it, and the possibility that he ever entertains anything like the impetus theory is often not noticed. In Leibniz, however, the idea has a very strong presence. He refers to the 'force by which bodies actually act on one another ... that [force] which is connected to motion ... and which, in turn, tends further to produce ... motion' (AG 120).

It cannot be stressed too much that this notion of a force as impetus to motion, and which is there in Descartes' and Leibniz's philosophies of nature, is crucially different from the modern notion of force which derives from Newton's *Principles of Natural Philosophy*. Newtonian dynamics has no place for a force which would cause a moving body to *keep on* moving. The 'force' in Newton's *Principles* is something which explains *change* of motion (acceleration or deceleration), not its steady continuation. It is a force which brings about an increase or decrease of a body's motion (or a change in its direction). Once such a change has come about there is, in Newton's scheme, no force sustaining a body in its new way. According to Leibniz, however, there is a 'motive force' which underlies uniform non-accelerated motion. As he conceives things, an increase in motion is due to an increase in a force already sustaining it; for Newton an increase is due to a new force, not to an increase in one already there.

For both Leibniz and Descartes before him the sustaining force of motion is transferred and redistributed in the collisions which, according to the mechanical philosophy, are what the physical world ultimately consists in. So, for example, when a moving body, A, collides with a stationary one, B, and gets it to move, at least some of A's moving force is transferred to B. Leibniz and Descartes both think, furthermore, that in the universe as a whole the total amount of this force remains a constant. But Leibniz was in complete disagreement with Descartes about how it is to be measured and quantified.

Central in Descartes' philosophy of nature was the notion of 'quantity of motion'. The 'motion' possessed by a chunk of matter, such as a billiard ball, is partly a straightforward matter of the speed at which it is moving: double the speed and there is twice as much motion. The quantity of motion cannot just be a matter of speed, however. With two equal balls moving at the same speed there must be more motion (twice) than with only one. Similarly a larger ball moving at a given speed must have more motion than a smaller one moving at that same speed (twice as much if the larger ball is twice the size of the smaller). So, Descartes concluded and passed on to his followers, the 'motion' of a moving body is to be measured by its size multiplied by speed: 'if one part of matter moves twice as fast as another which is twice as large, we must consider that there is the same quantity of motion in each part' (CSM 1.240).

The Cartesians quite naturally supposed that the measure of a sustaining force of motion must be the same as that of the quantity of motion being sustained by that force. The force sustaining the motion of a body of 2 units size and 2 units speed must be twice that of a body of 2 units size and 1 unit speed, and four times that of a body of 1 unit size and 1 unit speed. But one of the more prominent things in Leibniz's writings on these matters is the insistence that Descartes has gone completely astray here. Leibniz very plausibly argued that the force of a moving body is to be measured by the effect that the motion of the body can bring about in expending itself. It is to be measured by, for example, the vertical height to which a body can be raised by its motion as it rolls up a slope. It turns out, however, that though this height is directly proportional to the body's *size* it is not directly proportional to its *speed*. It follows that motive force is not to be measured in the Cartesian fashion, by the quantity of a body's motion, its size multiplied by its speed. (For Leibniz's proof of this see Note I at the end of this chapter.)

In fact the vertical height to which the motion of a body can take it is proportional to the *square* of the speed. As Leibniz said a decade after he had originally propounded his argument against Descartes: 'one can conclude ... that the forces in bodies are jointly proportional to the size of the bodies and the squares of the speeds' (AG 128). Having realized this, Leibniz began to express motive force, or *vis viva*, as the product of a body's size and the square of its speed. Expressed in this way, it contrasts nicely with Descartes' quantity of motion, the product of a body's size and its speed. Leibniz's argument that the 'force' of a body's motion is proportional not to its speed but to the square of its speed provoked the so-called '*vis viva* controversy', which continued well on into the next century.

Leibniz had a further objection to Cartesian thinking about 'quantity of motion'. Descartes believed that though 'quantity of motion' was redistributed in collisions between bodies it was never destroyed. The amount lost by one body must, he thought, be equal to the amount gained by the other. However, so Leibniz knew from a paper published by Huygens in 1669, Cartesian motion actually is not conserved in collisions. On the other hand, as Leibniz also learnt from Huygens, the quantity mv^2 (in effect, motive force measured in his way) *is* conserved in such collisions. (For Huygens's reasoning see Note II at the end of this chapter.)

There was something yet further which Huygens showed and which was of great interest to Leibniz. There is also conserved in collisions a quantity which at the time was called 'direction' or 'quantity of progress', but which is now called 'momentum'. It would be easy to confuse this with Descartes' 'quantity of motion', but in reality it is significantly different from it. It is like Cartesian motion in that a body's momentum depends partly on its size. It is like it too in that it has some relation to a body's speed. But it is unlike it in that it depends not just on the *speed* at which the body is moving, but on its *directed speed*, what is now known as *velocity*. Unlike speed, which is what is known as a scalar non-directional quantity, velocity is a vectorial directed quantity. A body going backwards at the same *speed* (say 2 units) as it was earlier going forwards has a changed *velocity* (from plus 2 to minus 2 units). Even if the speed of a car travelling round a circular track is constant, its velocity, relative to some given direction, is constantly changing. So even if a collision does not conserve undirected Cartesian motion it does conserve 'directed motion' or momentum. (For an example of this see Note III at the end of this chapter.)

Descartes' picture was that God 'always preserves the same quantity of motion' among bodies in the world, so that 'if one part slows down, we must suppose that some other part of equal size speeds up by the same amount' (CSM 1.240). At first sight this is very plausible. The world according to the mechanical philosophy is one in which corporeal matter is not static, but in which moving chunks of matter of various sizes collide with each other and move away at various speeds. It seems reasonable to suppose that in this world the sum total of all this motion should neither increase nor decrease. But that supposition allows of worlds which seem implausible, for example a world in which all matter was first moving in one direction and then, with unchanged speed, all moving in another. This would be a world in which the quantity of Cartesian motion had remained constant; so to rule it out something more than the constancy of mere Cartesian motion is required. So Leibniz came to see that what was a constant was not the sum total merely of the motion of bodies (the sum of their sizes multiplied by their speeds), but rather the sum total of their motion *in any given direction*.

A world in which all matter first moved in one direction and then, with unchanged speed, in the other, would be ruled out by this.

But does this really matter much? Couldn't a Cartesian easily allow that there was certainly something wrong with Descartes' picture as straightforwardly presented, but suggest that the error is marginal? Wouldn't it be a small matter just to redefine 'quantity of motion' as size multiplied, not now by speed, but by directed speed, by velocity? Doesn't it, after all, require only a simple change to Descartes' law of the conservation of motion, to say that it should be understood as applying to directed motion (i.e. momentum)?

Malebranche was inclined to think along these lines. Indeed he was very reluctant at first to see anything at all in Leibniz's criticisms of the ideas that Cartesian motion could be a measure of motive force, and that it was a conserved quantity. It took him some years to acknowledge there was anything in what Leibniz urged on him about the principle of the conservation of motion being false when motion was taken 'absolutely', with no account of direction. Even then his recognition was not whole-hearted. Descartes, he suggested, was guilty of no more than an ambiguity: Descartes' principle was nevertheless true when motion was taken 'relatively', with direction taken into account.

Malebranche certainly did not accept Leibniz's proposals as to the true measure of motive force. Indeed, since momentum, directed motion, *is* conserved in collisions, why couldn't *Leibniz* accept *it* rather than his own *vis viva* as the measure of force? Leibniz had a very good reason for not doing so, however. The fact is that momentum *is not an absolute* quantity whereas *vis viva* is.

The total amount of 'progress' or 'momentum' in a system of bodies is not necessarily changed by a change in the size or speed of those bodies. So, the total momentum in a system of two bodies of equal size and equal and opposite speed is *unchanged* from zero by a change in the bodies' size and speed *when they are changed equally*. For example, the total momentum is not increased from zero if their speeds are both doubled. What a change in the total amount of momentum requires is a change in the size or speed of the bodies *relative to each other*. For example, doubling the speed of just *one* of the bodies results in a change of total momentum from zero to one in the direction of movement of the larger body.

Results such as these clearly do not sit easily with the basic intuition that the amount of 'motion' (or its underlying force) is surely a function of the size and speed of the moving bodies, and would be increased by increases in either. It is no wonder that some Cartesians remained faithful to their master's measure of motion. For, quite in accord with their basic intuition, the total amount of Cartesian motion in a system of two bodies of equal size and equal and opposite speed is (unlike momentum) *not* zero, and it would (unlike momentum) be doubled by a doubling in speed of each body. Nevertheless, such Cartesians, faithful to one element of their master's teaching, had still to reject another element and acknowledge that Cartesian motion is not necessarily conserved in collisions.

Note I: Leibniz took it for granted that a falling body acquires the same amount of motive force as would be required to raise it back to its original height. He also took it that the force required to raise a one-pound body by four feet is the same as is required to raise a four-pound body by one foot. It follows from these assumptions that when it falls four feet a one-pound body acquires the same amount of force as a four-pound body acquires in falling one foot. Now, do these two bodies, which after their respective falls have the same amount of motive force, also have the same quantity of Cartesian motion?

Leibniz showed that they do not, by using some results obtained by Galileo who had studied the falling of bodies under the action of gravity. According to these, the speed acquired by a body in a four-foot fall will not be four times but only twice that acquired in a one-foot fall. So at the end of its fall the speed of a one-pound body is only twice the speed of a four-times-larger four-pound body. It therefore has only *half* the Cartesian motion of the larger. Hence, since, as agreed, the motive forces of the two bodies are the same, it follows that Cartesian motion cannot, contrary to the Cartesians, be the measure of motive force.

Note II: Huygens considered how various collisions between bodies of different sizes and different speeds would appear to two differently placed observers, one on a moving barge on which the collisions took place, and the other a stationary observer on the river bank. Using this imaginative device Huygens was able to show that to an extent Descartes was right: the amount of motion of one body in a collision could change only if there was some change in the motion of the other. But Descartes was wrong that these changes must be equal. Huygens showed that when a perfectly elastic hard body, A, of unit size which is moving with 3 units of speed hits a stationary body, B, twice its size, it will rebound from B with 1 unit of speed and move it forwards with 2 units. It therefore loses 2 units of the Cartesian quantity of motion while the other gains four.

Huygens also showed that there are various other conservations and regularities in collisions between perfectly elastic bodies. He showed that in a collision between two bodies the speed of their mutual approach is always the same as the speed of their mutual separation (in the example in the previous paragraph, 3 units). He also showed (as mentioned in the main text above) that the quantity mv^2 (in effect, motive force according to Leibniz's measure of it) is, unlike Cartesian motion, conserved in such collisions. (In the example of the previous paragraph, the combined force of A and B is $(1 \times 3^2) + (2 \times 0^2)$, i.e. 9, before the collision, and $(1 \times 1^2) + (2 \times 2^2)$, i.e. 9, after.)

Note III: The collision described in the previous note does not conserve undirected Cartesian motion but does conserve 'directed motion' or momentum. With speeds measured in the direction of A's initial motion, the total amount of momentum before the collision is 1×3 (for A) $+ 2 \times 0$ (for B), i.e. 3, and -1×1 (for A) $+ 2 \times 2$ (for B), i.e. 3 after the collision.

FURTHER READING

For more on the mechanical philosophy and what it displaced see Alexander (1985: ch. 2), Dijksterhuis (1961: ch. 3F, G), Hall (1960), Woolhouse (1983: 104–14).

Leibniz's dissatisfaction with physical matter as understood as mere extension is discussed in Bernstein (1981), Broad (1975: ch. 3.4), Buchdahl (1969: 406–24), Nason (1946).

For more on the impetus theory of motion see Clagett (1959: 521ff).

For further discussion of Huygens and the question of the measurement of force in the *vis viva* controversy see Dugas (1958, 280ff), Garber (1995: 309–21), Iltis (1971, 1973a, 1973b), Papineau (1977), Westfall (1971: 147ff).

CHAPTER 7

CAUSATION AND THE METAPHYSICS OF FORCE

i. MOTION

As described in the previous chapter, the 'mechanical philosophy' of the seventeenth century conceived of the physical world as consisting basically of matter in motion, motion sustained by a 'force of motion'. Collisions between material bodies were supposed to involve a transfer of motion, or its associated motive force, from one body to another, under the constraint that the total amount of 'motion' is constant.

It was generally agreed that though a stationary body could be put in motion by the impact of an already moving body, a stationary body could not put itself into motion. Bodies were not of themselves 'active'. In this respect they were seen as different from minds. A common idea was that immaterial minds are active, while material bodies are passive. Minds are able to initiate change and motion, both in themselves and in bodies. Bodies, however, lack self-movement. They can merely receive motion (whether from a mind or another body), motion which they retain or pass on to another body. This idea is there in an early letter from Leibniz: 'mind ... supplies motion to matter. For matter by itself is devoid of motion. For the origin of all motion is mind as Aristotle rightly saw' (La 643).

Against the background of this general understanding various questions were raised about motion, motive force and their transference from one body to another. The English philosopher John Toland reported on some of the puzzles people had 'about the moving force itself': 'what sort of being it is; where it resides, in matter or without it; by what means it can move matter; how it passes from one body to another ... and a thousand more such riddles' (Toland 1704: 156–7).

Descartes' position on these matters was not clear. On the one hand he often seems not to have been much troubled by the puzzles Toland raised about whether the force of motion 'resides in matter or without it', about 'how it passes from one body to another'. At times he says quite simply, and leaves it there, that it is 'mutually transferred when collisions occur' (CSM 1.243). But it is also possible to find in Descartes the idea that 'the force which impels' (K 258), the 'power causing motion' (K 257), not only has its origin in the divine mind, in God, but also that it resides there, and not in a moving body.

This idea that motion originates in and is sustained by God was maintained quite explicitly by Malebranche. It is, of course, part of his 'occasionalism' (which we encountered in Chapter 3) according to which there is no real or efficacious causation in the created world, God being the only real cause. This same idea is quite explicit too in Descartes' earlier followers, Gerauld de Cordemoy and Louis de La Forge. It is against 'the Cartesians', rather than Descartes himself, that Leibniz reacts in his rejections of 'occasionalism'.

ii. FROM OCCASIONALISM TO PRE-ESTABLISHED HARMONY

Malebranche took from Descartes the view that the continued existence of a body has to be understood as its constant re-creation by God; and it was a short step from there to supposing that a moving body was simply one which was re-created in a series of different places. It is in this way that the force of motion resides in God: 'the moving force of a body [is] ... simply the efficacy of the volition of God who conserves it differently in different places' (Malebranche 1688: 159). The idea that there is 'a certain force ... in the body moved and that is the cause of its motion' (Malebranche 1674–1675: 37) is quite wrong, Malebranche said: a moving body is sustained in its motion by the power of God. Similarly, contact with a moving body is not the real cause of the motion of a previously stationary body; it is merely the 'occasion' for God to produce motion in it. Malebranche allowed that we might still speak of a moving body's being 'the natural cause of the motion it communicates' when it comes into contact with a stationary body, but we must not lose sight of the true facts: 'A natural cause is ... not a real and true but only an occasional cause, which determines the Author of nature to act in such and such a manner in such and such a situation' (Malebranche 1674–1675: 448).

In his early twenties, at about the time Cordemoy and La Forge were publishing their ideas, Leibniz in fact agreed with much of what occasionalism held about motion. He wrote then that 'matter by itself is devoid of motion' (La 643); and that 'the origin of all motion is mind' (La 643). He went on to say what Malebranche himself was later to say: 'motion is not given in bodies as a real entity in them … whatever moves is continually recreated' (La 648). In later years however, as we saw in Chapters 3 and 6, he held very strongly that moving bodies do have an internal moving force. The process of this change of view, which did not involve a total break with occasionalism, was as follows.

Malebranche argued that moving bodies are not causally active. They cannot keep themselves in motion nor can they move others. He then argued (as we will see in the next chapter) that the *human* mind is not causally active either. So, he concluded, God alone has force and is active. In a letter of 1679 Leibniz wholeheartedly agreed with Malebranche about the first part of this: 'I am entirely of your opinion', he said, 'concerning the impossibility of conceiving that a substance which has nothing but extension, without thought, can act' (L 209). Then, a few months later he wrote: 'I approve most heartily … [what] you advance … that strictly speaking, bodies do not act' (L 210). But Leibniz disagreed with Malebranche's conclusion that only God possesses activity and force. Malebranche had not traced things back to first principles, he said. Malebranche had failed to see that the impossibility of bodies being causally active follows from 'certain axioms', axioms which Leibniz did 'not as yet see used anywhere' (L 210). Malebranche's denial of bodies' causal activity had, Leibniz argued, 'gone only halfway' (L 209).

What Malebranche had not seen was that one of the 'important reasons' (L 210) there are for denying that body can act (namely that there is no activity or force in extension as such) also shows that 'matter is something different from mere extension' (L 209). Malebranche denied that body has any force or activity because, as he quite correctly saw, this follows from what he had learnt from Descartes, that body is merely extension. But he should have argued the other way, Leibniz said. He should have seen that he was 'depending on a false principle, and that the notion of body from which such consequences were derived had been improperly explicated' (AG 130). On the assumption that bodies are merely extended, they do indeed have no activity and force. But what this really shows, Leibniz said, is that there must be something more than extension to the nature of material substance, something which provides activity and force. What this is has been explained in Chapter 3.

To Malebranche's mind it was an irreligious and pagan error to think that anything other than God could exercise any force or be active. 'Our idea of cause or of power to act ... represents something divine' (Malebranche 1674–1675: 446). According to Malebranche, we fail to do justice to God's supreme divinity when we suppose that anything other than God could be a real cause with power to act. Leibniz thought quite differently. He thought it would be a complete indignity for God to be the sole cause of events in the created world, to be always acting in 'extraordinary concourse' with it. For Leibniz it would have been far more worthy of God to have created things which themselves are active and productive of their changes.

In his *Historical and Critical Dictionary* Pierre Bayle agreed that Leibniz's conception of the created world and of God's relation to it did far more justice to God's power, wisdom and intelligence than did Malebranche's. He did not agree, however, when Leibniz sometimes described the dealings with the world which the occasionalists attributed to God, not only as being undignified of God, but as involving miracles.

Just because all change in the world is due to God's activity there is no reason to think that this involves miracles, Bayle said. According to occasionalism God acts 'only according to general laws' (Bayle 1696: 74), so there is no question of his acting miraculously. Occasionalists do not hold that God decides on each occasion how bodies should move after a collision. They hold that God makes a single, general, decision, makes up his mind once and for all, about the laws of motion. So it is wrong to say that miracles are involved in his activity; for a miracle, Bayle said, is something produced by God 'as an exception to general laws, and [...] anything he does immediately according to ... [general] laws is not, properly speaking, a miracle' (Bayle 1702: 87).

But Leibniz's view of miracles was different from Bayle's. According to Leibniz the results of God's actions would still be miracles even if those actions were quite regular and in accordance with perfectly general decisions. We cannot reason that since God acts 'only according to a general rule he acts without miracles'. Supposing God decided 'to carry out a certain action every time that a certain circumstance occurred, this action would still be a miracle, although perfectly ordinary' (LA 92–3). Leibniz did not think that a miracle is necessarily something that is unusual or out of the ordinary. The frequency and regularity, the lawlikeness of events, is, to his way of thinking, of no relevance to the question of their being miracles or not. What makes something a miracle is, quite simply, that it results from God rather than from the natures of the things involved. 'It isn't sufficient to say that God has made a general law', Leibniz insisted, 'for in addition to the decree there has also to be a natural way of carrying it out. It is necessary, that is, that what happens should be explicable in terms of the God-given nature of things' (WF 82). If what happened in the world were a direct result of God's power and activity, and not of any power or force on the part of created things themselves, then, for Leibniz, those happenings, no matter how regular and law-like they may be, would be miracles. 'The distinguishing mark of miracles … is that they cannot be accounted for by the natures of created things' (T 257). The occasionalists, he said, 'introduce a miracle which is no less one for being continual … A miracle differs intrinsically … from an ordinary action, and not by an external accident of frequent repetition' (LA 93).

Leibniz's position is clear. What would make the ordinary, regular course of events non-miraculous is not simply that it be the ordinary, regular course. How those events come about is relevant too. To be non-miraculous they must happen as they do, not because of God's action on the world, but because the things in it are active substances whose nature it is to do as they do.

When Bayle pointed out that it is not part of occasionalism that God decides anew on each occasion how, for example, to move a pair of bodies after colliding them, there was something he left unclear. The idea that God acts according to general rules which he has decided on once and for all, and so does not *decide* on each occasion, leaves open whether he needs to *act* on each occasion. Even if God were to decide once and for all, and as a perfectly general matter, to do *this* kind of thing on the occasion of *that*, might he not, on each particular occasion, still need to *do* something?

Arnauld was clearer than Bayle about this. On his account of it, occasionalism holds that, having antecedently made a general decision about what kind of event should follow what, God does *not* have to do anything further on each particular occasion. Arnauld explained that what the occasionalists claim is that God causes things to happen 'by a single act of the eternal will, by which he chooses to do all which it would be necessary to do, in order that the universe might be what he wanted it to be' (LA 84). They do not claim that God causes things to happen by a new act of will on each new occasion.

Leibniz thought that this conception of things was incoherent. God's making general decisions is, by itself, not enough, was his view. The mere making of a decision does not of itself ensure that the decision will be carried out. Not even divine decisions are self-fulfilling; even they need to be put into effect. Some means are necessary by which they are carried out. Either God must implement his own laws himself, and must act in accordance with them when the occasion arises it; or angels must be 'expressly charged' with this responsibility (WF 82); or, as Leibniz held was the case, created substances must themselves have 'tools for doing so' (WF 116) and there must be set up a 'natural way of carrying ... out' (WF 82) God's decisions and laws.

Leibniz's position about this comes out again in his discussion of the occasionalist, Johann Sturm. According to Sturm, Leibniz reported, 'motions which take place now come about as the result of an *eternal law* which God has set up, a law which he [Sturm] then calls a volition and a *command*'. Accordingly, 'there is no need for a new divine command, a new volition' (NI 158) on God's part. Sturm 'rejects the view that God moves a thing like a woodcutter moves an ax' (NI 5), and held that events happen as they do solely as a result of this past decision.

Leibniz could not accept this. Since 'that past command does not now exist, it cannot now bring anything about unless it left behind some subsistent effect at the time, an effect which even now endures and now is at work'. What is required is that

> by his command things were formed in such a way that they were rendered appropriate for fulfilling the will of the command ... [W]e must admit that a certain efficacy has been placed in things, a form or force ... something from which the series of phenomena follows in accordance with the prescript of the first command. (NI 6)

In a summary of what he thought about occasionalism Leibniz wrote: 'The system of occasional causes must be partly admitted and partly rejected' (PM 80). It goes wrong in holding that all activity and power is concentrated in God; for, on the contrary, there *is*, Leibniz insists, power and activity in the created world. 'Each substance is the true and real cause of its *immanent* actions and has the power of acting' (PM 80). But this causation in the world is *internal* (immanent) to each substance, and so occasionalism is right, in holding that created substances have no power or force to act *on each other*. '[E]ach substance (with the sole exception of God) is only the occasional cause of those of its actions which are *transient* [transitive] with regard to another substance' (PM 81). The occasionalists are right in their rejection of causality *between* created substances. But it is 'as distant as it could possibly be from reason' to go further, as the occasionalists do, and to reject 'the *immanent* [*internal*] *actions* of substances' (NI 10) too.

Malebranche was right, Leibniz agrees, to hold that created things do not interact with and affect each other. But he was wrong to conclude that therefore all activity and force resides in God, wrong that all changes in the world are due to God. It is rather, Leibniz insists, that each created thing brings about *its own* changes. Despite this difference between the two sides there is an important similarity, however. According to the occasionalists it is not just that God brings about the changes in one created thing, it is rather that he brings them about *on the occasion of* changes in other created things. Similarly, it is part of Leibniz's view not just that there are self-generated changes in each created thing, it is rather that changes in one created thing in effect occur *on the occasion of* the *self-generated* changes in another. This crucial feature (and others) of his 'pre-established harmony' theory of causation will be discussed further in Chapter 8 in connection with the 'causation' between body and mind.

FURTHER READING

For Malebranche's occasionalism, and Leibniz's objections to it see Jolley (2005), Loeb (1981: ch. 5), McRae (1985), Rutherford (1993), Sleigh (1990b).

On pre-established harmony and Leibniz's denial of causal interaction see Ishiguro (1977), Loeb (1981: ch. 7), O'Neill (1993), Woolhouse (1985).

BODY AND MIND

i. BODILY DEATH

Chapters 3, 4 and 5 have traced two of Leibniz's views about corporeal substances: a realism and an idealism. Generally speaking, on either account corporeal substances are in some way a unified combination of an animating mental entelechy and a body. According to the 'realist' view, they consist of a substantial form and a material body, a material body which consists of smaller corporeal substances. According to the 'idealist' view, they consist of a chief monad which 'dominates' an aggregate of other monads which constitutes the foundation of the phenomenon of its body. In each case both the mental entelechy and the combination of which it is a part are substances, whereas on neither account is the body taken by itself a substance. Standing back from the undoubted differences between these two views there is more to be said about the relation between body and mind.

Descartes believed that the immaterial mind or soul could exist apart from a corporeal body. He spoke of the mind's being 'newly united to an infant's body' and of the mind's being 'taken out of the prison of the body' (K 111). Leibniz held, however, that there are never any minds or souls which are not embodied in some matter and so part of a corporeal substance: there is, he said, 'naturally no soul without an animate body' (LA 124). He also believed, as we saw in Chapter 5, that there were different kinds of minds or soul which differed accordingly as they were reflexively conscious (souls, properly speaking), non-reflexively conscious (animal souls) or unconscious (bare monads). This gave a particular slant to his account of birth, death and immortality, an account which differs from both Descartes' and some popular ideas.

Descartes' belief that non-human animals are nothing more than complex mechanisms, lacking feeling and sensation, was at least partially theologically motivated. It was generally supposed that immaterial souls were indestructible (unless by God) and so immortal. We see this idea at work in Leibniz when he says that monads 'can only begin by creation and end by annihilation' (Mon 6). But now, if non-human animals are *not* just insensate machines, and have immaterial souls, might they not have a place in heaven too? On the other hand if souls are not immortal, then, as Descartes worried, 'after this present life we have nothing to fear or to hope for, any more than flies or ants' (CSM 1.141). According to Leibniz, the Cartesian opinion that 'it is only man who truly has a soul and, indeed, who has perception and appetite' was something which 'will never receive general approval'. It was 'rushed into' because 'it seemed necessary either to ascribe immortal souls to beasts or to admit that the soul of man could be mortal' (L 588).

In thinking about immortality for the soul the Cartesians were of course thinking about its survival after bodily death. But what exactly did they understand by 'death'? The 'death' of a purely mechanical non-human animal was understood as akin to the running down of a clock or to its stopping because of wear and tear. The death of a human was understood in the same way. It was not that the machine of the body 'dies' as a consequence of the soul's leaving and ceasing to animate it; it was rather the other way around: first, the body dies or breaks down, and then, as a consequence, the soul leaves it. It is not, Descartes explained, that death occurs 'through the absence of the soul'; it occurs 'because one of the principal parts of the body decays'. The difference between a living human body and a human corpse is like that between 'a watch ... when it is wound up' and 'the same watch or machine when it is broken' (CSM 1.329–30).

Now Leibniz, we have seen, was not shy of asserting that humans are not the only creatures with immaterial and indestructible souls. Along with humans 'I include the beasts and believe that they too have sense, and souls which are properly described as immaterial and are ... imperishable' (NE 67). Indeed he did this enthusiastically, holding that there are infinitely more kinds of animated beings than we think, and that the world is populated with 'animals' within 'animals'. This was so whether we are thinking of the world during his 'middle' period, the world of real corporeal substances, or the later idealist world of the *Monadology*. In both cases 'there is a world of creatures ... in the smallest portion of matter' (Mon 66).

Leibniz's belief that there is a world of small animated creatures in the smallest part of matter was sustained by the work of the Dutch biologist John Swammerdam and the microscopists Nicholas Hartsoeker, Marcello Malpighi and Anton van Leeuwenhoek. This work also encouraged him in a belief in pre-formationism, a belief to the effect that the generation of animals is a matter of development and augmentation of a pre-formed creature. Birth and death, he thought, are not what we usually think. There is 'no first birth or entirely new generation of an animal ... no final extinction or complete death' (NS 14).

These beliefs would, Leibniz thought, have helped the Cartesians cut through their difficulty that if animals had souls and were immortal those souls would need to exist apart from matter as surely ours do. What had not occurred to them, Leibniz thought, was that death (even in the human case) is not separation of an immaterial soul from a body. Immortality is not a matter of the survival of a detached soul. The Cartesians' failure was to have not 'hit on the idea of the preservation of the animal in miniature' (NE 67).

Leibniz's correspondent Arnauld shared something of the Cartesians' perplexity. Beginning to realize that Leibniz's position was that all living creatures had souls he saw some difficulty in it. What is the fate of all these souls after death? He conjured up the picture of a destructive fire at a silkworm farm. What, he asked, 'would become of those one hundred thousand indestructible souls? Would they subsist while separated from all matter, like our souls?' (LA 87–8). Arnauld's question was based on a false presupposition of course. Leibniz did not even hold that after death *our* souls 'exist separated from all matter' so he certainly did not hold that silkworm souls do. There are no forms or entelechies that are not embodied in matter and are not elements of a corporeal substance.

At death a soul does not totally separate from a body, leaving it to moulder away. Rather, the soul remains embodied in at least some part of the body. There is never 'strictly speaking, complete death, involving the separation of the soul'; instead there are only bodily 'envelopments and diminutions' (Mon 73). Death is a matter of bodily 'transformation', a 'diminution and encapsulation of an animal which nevertheless still subsists and remains living and organised' (LA 123). If an animal, human or otherwise, were torn apart and destroyed, its 'soul' will remain 'in a certain part which is still alive' (LA 100). Furthermore, though God could destroy souls, they are in themselves 'indestructible by natural means' (LA 76), and 'always continue to exist' (NS 12).

Leibniz was perfectly clear that at death an ordinary brute animal 'sink[s] down ... into a world of little creatures among which its perceptions are more limited' (LA 99). But there is some equivocation as to what happens when humans 'die'. Often it seems that humans too go through these same bodily transformations and diminutions, falling for a time into an unconscious 'swoon' or 'sleep', awaiting Judgement Day. Yet Leibniz also spoke as though our bodies are not subject to transformations of the same kind as those of other animals. Rational minds 'are not subject to these cycles' (LA 99–100), he said. As though forgetting his official view that souls are 'never entirely without a body', he said at one point that at death, God 'separates [human minds] from bodies'. But then, remembering himself, he added as a parenthetical afterthought, that the separation is 'at least from their grosser bodies' (LA 100).

The idea here is that after 'death' human souls are associated for a time with some rarefied material body. 'For why cannot the soul always retain a subtle body organized after its own manner, which could even some day reassume the form of its visible body in the resurrection?'. Such a 'glorified body' is often attributed 'to the blessed', and the early Church Fathers have attributed 'a subtle body to angels' (L 556–7). Presumably the thought behind this need for human souls to be free from a coarse body is that, pending the resurrection, they need to retain their distinctly human properties of memory and self-consciousness – something they could not do if they were associated with some small, quite inappropriately organized part of a corrupting corpse. Indeed though no soul ever ceases to exist it is only human souls which are, in Leibniz's strict use of the term, 'immortal'. Only they have the moral identity which fits them for Divine reward and punishment. Other souls are said to be 'ceaseless' (NE 236).

Just as the 'death' of human beings with their rational souls is treated differently from that of other animals, so too is their 'birth'. Animal souls have existed since the creation of the world.

The generation of all animals which are deprived of reason, which do not require a new act of creation, is only the transformation of another animal which is already alive, but which is often imperceptible ... [A]nimal souls ... have been created from the beginning of the world. (LA 75)

As for the rational soul, however, Leibniz is unsure. Perhaps God produces it 'only when the animated body which exists in the seed proceeds to take on human form'. In which case the now displaced and primitive soul of the spermatic animal will be annihilated. Perhaps, alternatively, there is some 'natural means' by which a merely sentient soul can be raised 'to the degree of a reasoning soul' (T 173). Leibniz finds this 'difficult to imagine' (T 173), and thinks it more likely that there is some 'special operation ... a kind of *transcreation*' (T 193), by which God 'through his extraordinary influence' transmutes the one soul into the other, by giving it the perfection of rationality (LA 72–3).

ii. UNION OF MIND AND BODY: DESCARTES AND MALEBRANCHE

A frequently discussed question in the seventeenth century was that of the relation between mind and body: what exactly is the nature of their connection and union? Something was said about this in Chapter 5 in specific connection with Leibniz's idealist account of body, but there is more to be said by way of putting that in a wider and more general context.

How the two things are related is something which we might naturally ask ourselves. We believe ourselves to have both a mind and a body, and believe that there is a close relation, a union between the two. For example, having decided to move our hand we can move it; and, in the other direction, the puncturing of its flesh will produce a sensation of pain. As Descartes put it:

people who never philosophize and use only their senses have no doubt that the soul moves the body and that the body acts on the soul ... Everyone feels that he is a single person with both body and thought so related by nature that the thought can move the body and feel the things which happen to it. (K 141–2)

Leibniz's view of the matter is best located, as so often, by reference to those of Descartes and of the Cartesian occasionalists. Just as his account of substance was explicitly formulated in contrast to theirs, so too was his account of the relation between mind and body. The view with which Descartes is usually associated is built on his doctrine that there are two kinds of substances: mental thinking substance or mind, and material extended substance or body. As we have seen on more than one occasion, Leibniz did not share Descartes' dualism: considered apart from a mind, the body was not a substance for him. In the present context, however, he did as he often did, and adjusted his language to fit with that of others, and spoke as though the question concerned the relation between two different substances.

A human being, for Descartes, is some kind of union of two different substances, mind and body. One aspect of this union is causal interaction between the two. According to the detailed physiological theory which Descartes developed, the interaction between the body and the mind took place in a certain part of the brain, the pineal gland: 'the mind is not immediately affected by all parts of the body, but only by ... one small part of the brain' (CSM 2.59).

This view that the relationship between mind and body involves there being a causal connection between the two has always been thought to be problematic. Many people have wondered, both in Descartes' time and later, how substances of essentially different kinds, such as Descartes holds body and mind to be, can possibly causally interact. How can an unthinking substance cause sensations in a thinking substance? How can an unextended substance cause motion in an extended substance? Descartes' contemporary, Pierre Gassendi could not see how, in the case of unextended mind, there could be 'any influence exerted upon a thing and any motion in it without mutual contact between the mover and the moved' (Gassendi 1644: 273). Nor, in the other direction, could he see how 'an unextended subject ... could receive the semblance or idea of a body that is extended' (CSM 2.234). As a result he was inclined towards a thoroughgoing materialism, and to reject such entities as Cartesian immaterial minds. Locke was sympathetic to Gassendi's worries: '[w]e cannot conceive how anything but impulse of body can move body'. But he was in no doubt that 'constant experience' *does* show that voluntary motions *can* be produced in our bodies by nothing more than 'the free action or thought of our minds' (Locke 1690: 4.10.19).

It is perhaps somewhat surprising, then, that Descartes himself was quite sanguine about all of this. He told Gassendi that it 'cannot in any way be proved' that 'if the soul and the body are two substances whose nature is different, this prevents them from being able to act on each other' (CSM 2.275). Similarly his follower Louis de La Forge said it was simply an 'unhappy prejudice' (La Forge 1666: 236) to suppose that for the soul to move the body it would need to be material itself, and so able to be in literal contact with it.

Now Leibniz's view about the 'union' of body and mind was worked out not just in reaction to Descartes', but in response to that of the occasionalists too. As we saw in Chapters 3 and 7, the occasionalists held that there is no real causal activity in the material world and that God is the real cause of all events there. So far as motion, one of the core features of the world according to the mechanical philosophy, was concerned, they argued: corporeal bodies cannot cause motion, so a mind or minds must be the cause of motion; finite human minds cannot cause motion in bodies; therefore God must be the cause of their motion. The second of these two premises, that finite minds cannot cause motion in bodies, clearly goes against Descartes' body/mind interactionism according to which the human mind can have a real effect on that part of the material world which is its own body.

As an occasionalist, Malebranche held that 'there is absolutely no mind created that can move a body as a true or principal cause, just as it has been said that no body could move itself'. In support of this he argued that when we consider what it is to be a finite, created mind 'we do not see any necessary connection between its will and the motion of any body whatsoever'. There seems no reason, he felt, why willing by a finite, limited mind should necessarily have any effect in the material world, such as the movement of a hand. By contrast, he says, when we consider that God is an infinitely perfect and all-powerful being, 'it is impossible to conceive that He wills a body to be moved and that this body not be moved' (Malebranche 1674–1675: 448).

We might agree with Malebranche here that there is no *necessary* or inevitable connection between our will and the movement of some body: we cannot get a billiard ball to move simply by willing it to move. We might allow too that the will of an all-perfect, all-powerful being could not fail to have effect. But why should it follow that a finite will cannot *ever* succeed? Why should we suppose that the movement of our hand is not the effect of our willing it?

Perhaps what Malebranche had in mind is something he says elsewhere about there being no connection between our finite will and events in the world. From a physical and physiological point of view the raising of an arm is a very complex matter, involving the contracting of muscles, impulses in the nerves, and so on. Following Descartes and the physiologists of his day Malebranche understood all of this in terms of the movements of what were called 'animal spirits', fluids running throughout the body, the equivalent of more recent nerve impulses. Now most of us are ignorant of these matters, and so, Malebranche reasoned, we actually do not know how to raise our arms. 'I see clearly', he said, 'that there can be no relation between the volition I have to move my arm and the agitation of the animal spirits' (Malebranche 1677–1678: 669).

iii. LEIBNIZ'S OBJECTIONS TO INTERACTIONISM AND OCCASIONALISM

To an extent Leibniz agreed with Malebranche's anti-Cartesian conclusion. Speaking of the 'great mystery' of the union of mind and body, he was clear that 'there is no way' of understanding how they could have any influence on each other (DM 33). His argument is quite different from Malebranche's, however, and applies just as much to the possibility of an infinite mind's having an effect in the corporeal world, as it does to a finite, limited mind's doing so. There is, he argued in his letters to Arnauld, no proportionality or commensurability between mind and body, no basis for any rule. There is nothing to determine 'what degree of speed a mind will give to a body'. What rational connection can there be between a mind's thoughts and 'the paths and angles of direction of [moving] bodies' (LA 93–4)?

Leibniz's point about the incommensurability of mind and body connects with things we have seen in Chapter 6. It concerns all minds, whether finite and limited, or infinite and omniscient. There is nothing wrong with the idea that, in terms of the speed and the direction of their motion, bodies are affected in their collisions with each other. But, Leibniz's thought was, the idea that an immaterial mind could affect the motion, the speed and the direction of a corporeal body, is wrong in principle. It is just not clear how one would begin to work out detailed rules relating mental volitions to the change in the speed and the direction of things in the material world.

This incommensurability comes out most clearly in the fact that the idea that the mind might produce motion in some part of the material world is, as Leibniz pointed out, inconsistent with Descartes' own physics. When my hand is caused to move by something which hits it then, according to Descartes' 'law' that there is a constant quantity of motion in the world, the quantity of motion the hand acquires is counterbalanced by corresponding loss of motion in the colliding object. But if my hand were caused to move by my willing it, the increase in its quantity of motion could not be counterbalanced by corresponding decrease in my mind. My mind is unextended and immaterial, and as such it has no size, or speed, and so no quantity of Cartesian motion. This supposed action of my mind on my body would therefore involve an increase in the total quantity of motion in the corporeal world. Descartes' belief that voluntary action is a matter of the mind acting causally on the body is, it would seem, inconsistent with his own 'law' of the conservation of the total quantity of motion.

Leibniz was not the first to argue that Descartes' interactionist account of the 'union' of body and mind was inconsistent with Cartesian physics. The occasionalist Gerauld de Cordemoy had done so earlier. But Leibniz made much use of the point in developing his own account of the 'union'. Indeed, he maintained that Descartes himself was conscious of and worried by the problem. Descartes, he said, 'believed in the conservation of the same quantity of motion in bodies ... [and] the changes which take place in the body as a consequence of modifications of the soul caused him some difficulty, because they seemed to break this law' (WF 51). Yet, apart from that remark, there is in fact no evidence available now that Descartes saw any problem here. One suggestion has been that while he certainly held that collisions *between bodies* cannot increase motion he may not have meant to deny that causal interaction *between mind and body* can increase it (Garber 1983: 115). Yet even if Descartes meant his law of conservation of motion to be restricted in this way, the action of mind on body would possibly be inconsistent with the stability of the material world. Cordemoy suggested that a certain quantity of motion may be required for the world to be as it is, and that the continual addition of motion by the action of human mind might destabilize it.

Even so, perhaps Descartes *did* see a problem and Leibniz (who had access to some of Descartes' manuscripts which have since been lost) knew something we do not. At any rate, he went on to say that Descartes 'thought he had found a solution'. This, as Leibniz reported it, was based on a distinction 'between motion and direction'. Given this distinction Descartes was, according to Leibniz, then able to say that though, consistently with the law of conservation of motion, the soul 'can neither increase or decrease the *moving force*', it 'does change *the direction or determination* of the course of the animal spirits: and this is how voluntary motion takes place' (WF 51).

Leibniz thought this was 'certainly ingenious'. Within the terms of Descartes' own philosophy of science it undoubtedly is a 'way out' of the problem. In his thinking about the laws of motion Descartes had from the very start made a distinction between the speed of a body's motion and the direction or determination of that motion. Moreover (as we saw in Chapter 6), 'quantity of motion', which is what is supposed to be constant in the Cartesian corporeal world, is a function of a body's scalar speed – that is, its speed in whatever direction it happens to be moving. The direction or determination of the motion is quite irrelevant to the quantity of motion. Similarly, changes of that direction do not mean changes to the quantity of motion. So the ability to determine and change the direction of motion is just what the mind needs to make itself felt in the corporeal world. Descartes' 'way out' allows both for the mind to cause changes in the body and for his law of the conservation of the total quantity of motion to hold without any restriction.

Yet just as we have no evidence that *Descartes* himself was ever troubled by the thought of an inconsistency of his account of the relation between mind and body with his physics, so we have none that he found this 'way out'. We know of nothing which could explain how Leibniz could say to Arnauld, that 'it seems Descartes wanted to say that the soul ... changes merely the direction or determination of the motion and not the force which is in bodies' (LA 117). Something like this story is true of Descartes' followers, however. Sixteen years after Descartes' death in 1664, La Forge taught that though 'the soul has no power to increase or decrease the motion of the [animal] spirits which leave the gland', it can *determine* them, that is to say, 'turn them in the direction where they need to go to execute its will' (La Forge 1666: 245–6). It can re-direct the motion that already exists, and so bring about different bodily movements.

Though Leibniz was impressed by the ingenuity of this Cartesian 'way out' he knew it actually did not save the Cartesian schema. We saw in Chapter 6 that Descartes' 'law' of the conservation of motion is false, and so not worth saving. But his point here is not that. What he has his mind on here is, rather, the reason why it is false – precisely because it takes no account of the direction of motion! Ironically, though Cartesian motion is *not* conserved, 'directed motion' or momentum *is*. As a result there is no scope at all for the mind to have any causal effect on the body. It can affect *neither* its speed *nor* the direction of its motion. This attempt to show how action of the mind could be consistent with the Cartesian conservation law just does not work, for, as Leibniz pointed out to Arnauld, 'there is in nature [a] ... general law which M. Descartes did not perceive ... namely that the sum total of direction or determination must always be a constant' (LA 94). The Cartesian 'ingenious way out', in pointlessly attempting to save a false 'law', is blocked by a true one!

Leibniz often repeated this argument against the Cartesian interactionist view of the 'union' of body and mind. He made clear that his own account of the relation between body and mind, what came to be called 'the system of pre-established harmony' (which we have yet to consider), was not open to it. He also claimed, proudly and boldly, that had Descartes known of the law of conservation of directed motion he would have come to Leibniz's own view.

If the (true) law of conservation of directed motion, or momentum, had been known in Descartes's day ... he would undoubtedly have been led to my system of pre-established harmony, for he would have recognized that it is just as reasonable to say that the soul does not change the quantity of the direction of the body as it is to deny to the soul the power of changing the quantity of its force, both being equally contrary to the order of things, and the laws of nature, since both are equally inexplicable. (L 587)

Bertrand Russell thought this was going too far (1900: 81). No doubt, he agreed, Descartes would have abandoned his interactionism; after all, his followers, such as Malebranche, abandoned it, and substituted for it their own theory. But why (Russell wondered) could not a knowledge of the law of conservation of momentum or directed motion have led Descartes just as easily to occasionalism as to Leibniz's theory? In fact, unremarked by Russell, Leibniz had already answered this question. Quite simply, the argument against Descartes' interactionism on the grounds of its inconsistency with physical conservation laws *applies equally against occasionalism*.

What is in effect Leibniz's answer to Russell is given in detail in his *Theodicy*: If Descartes had known that 'direction [momentum] is ... conserved', he would have 'recognised that without a complete derangement of the laws of Nature the soul could not act physically upon the body'; and, once he had recognized that, he would have been 'led direct to the Hypothesis of Pre-established Harmony'. But why? Why might he not have been led to occasionalism? Because, said Leibniz, one could not

> listen here to philosophers ... who produce a God ... to bring about the final solution of the piece, maintaining that God exerts himself deliberately to move bodies as the soul pleases and to give perceptions to the soul as the body requires.

But, again, why not? Just what is wrong with that as a solution? Because, Leibniz went on to explain, this system of occasional causes 'besides introducing perpetual miracles to establish communication between these two substances, does not obviate the derangement of ... natural laws' (T 156–7).

As the quotation makes clear, this objection to occasionalism is additional to the one already discussed in Chapter 6. That earlier one involved the claim that occasionalism involves miracles in replacing the activity of created substances by direct divine action on the material world. This further objection is that, quite apart from being miraculous, such action would be inconsistent with natural law. It would be inconsistent with the law of conservation of directed motion not merely for the mind to cause motion in the body but *even for God on the 'occasion'* of some volition in a mind to cause motion in the body. No matter how uniform and perfectly regular his actions are, it is inconsistent with natural law for God to act on the material world, by, for example, moving a person's arm on the 'occasion' of some desire or act of will in the person's mind. If the cause of a change in the motion of a body were a mental volition and not the impact of another body, then, *whether that cause be 'real' or 'occasional'*, the law of conservation of directed motion would be broken. In this respect, there is no advantage to occasionalism over interactionism. Though occasionalism differs from interactionism with respect to the metaphysics of causation, it effectively agrees with it in holding that, whether it is 'real' or 'occasional', there *is* causation between mind and body. Both theories allow that the material world is not closed to mental causation (be it 'real' or 'occasional'). As a consequence both are involved with bodily movements sometimes being not subject to otherwise true conservation laws. To avoid the point that an account of the union of mind and body must not involve the interruption of the laws of physics by mental events, there is nothing to be gained by the substitution of 'occasional' for 'real' causation. For Leibniz, the conclusion to draw is that mind and body are causally isolated from each other.

iv. PRE-ESTABLISHED HARMONY

So from the flaws, as he saw them, in interactionism and occasionalism Leibniz drew the conclusion that mind and body must be causally independent of each other, so that bodily effects always have bodily causes, and mental effects always mental causes. It is a conclusion which is a central feature of his own positive account of the 'union' between body and mind – an account which at first he called the 'hypothesis of concomitance' or of 'agreements', and then, eventually and most famously, 'the system of pre-established harmony'. It is, he says, an hypothesis which follows from his account of substance. As we saw in Chapter 7, Leibniz at first expressed partial agreement with Malebranche's occasionalist ideas. He agreed that *if* there were no more to material substance than extension (as Malebranche, following Descartes, thought) *then* (as Malebranche wanted to conclude) there could be no activity and no real causation in the material world. This in turn meant that there could be no interaction between finite minds and bodies. But Leibniz thought Malebranche had 'gone only half way'. Malebranche was right about what would be the case *if* matter were just extension; but he had failed to learn the right lesson from this, namely that matter *is not* just extension. Matter, Leibniz concluded, must be something more than passive extension, and must involve activity, substantial forms and entelechies. Though created things are not *inter*active, they are nevertheless *active*.

This conception is one which is developed at the time of the *Discourse on Metaphysics*, of course. It is the conception according to which a created substance is such that 'all its actions come from its own depths' (LA 136). It is, moreover, a conception by which, Leibniz says, we get an 'unexpected solution' of the 'great mystery of the union of soul and body' (DM 33).

What is this 'unexpected solution'? '[T]he true reason' of this union, Leibniz said, is this: since 'everything happening to the soul and to every substance is a consequence of its notion ... the very idea or essence of the soul makes all its appearances or perceptions arise spontaneously out of its own nature', and this happens in such a way that 'they answer of themselves to what happens ... in the body assigned to it' (DM 33). There is, that is to say, no causal inter-action between mind and body; yet though each is responsible for its own changes there is a correspondence between them.

According to Kant this doctrine of pre-established harmony between body and mind is 'the strangest figment ever to be excogi-tated by philosophy' (Kant 1804: 375). So far as changes in the body go, Leibniz held that they can be explained purely according to the principles of the mechanical philosophy, and without any reference to the mind. 'All the phenomena of bodies', he told Arnauld, 'can be explained mechanically ... without worrying about whether or not there are souls' (LA 78). When the bodies concerned are those of non-human animals, this claim is entirely in agreement with what Descartes held. For Descartes (as in Chapter 5), non-human animals are simply machines, like complex clocks. All their behavi-our can be explained in terms of the motions of matter. But Descartes thought differently about human animals. They are not just machines for him; some of their behaviour is voluntary and caused by their minds. According to a complete materialism such as that of Hobbes or Epicurus, however, Descartes was wrong about that. Materialism maintains that in no case is there an immaterial mind to affect the body, and human beings are purely mechanical too.

So the one half of Leibniz's hypothesis of pre-established harmoni-ous concomitance which concerns the body means that Cartesianism is only partially right and materialism is wholly so. Leibniz himself gave a nice summary of these dialectical relationships:

[E]verything happens in the body ... as if the wicked doctrine of those who ... believe that the soul is material were true; or as if man himself were only body, or an automaton. Thus the materialists have extended to man as well what the Cartesians maintain with regard to all other animals ... Those who point out to the Cartesians that the way they prove that animals are only *automata* could be taken as justifying someone who said that, metaphysically speaking, it is possible that all other men, except himself, are simple automata, have said exactly and precisely what I need for this half of my theory, which concerns the body (WF 112–13).

The other half of Leibniz's hypothesis of concomitance is that the mind is a 'spiritual automaton': all changes in it result from itself. All its perceptions 'arise spontaneously out of its nature' (DM 33). Again there is partial agreement with Descartes here, for he held that at least we *humans* have immaterial minds, and that at least *sometimes* our thoughts 'have the soul as their cause' (CSM 1.335). But there is some disagreement too, for Descartes held that *non-human animals* do not have minds, and he held that the mind is *not always* 'the source of its phenomena'. There is, of course, *complete* disagreement with the materialists for they hold that in no case is there an immaterial mind. But, Leibniz says, our own 'internal experience' of a perceiving ego refutes them. That internal experience of ourselves cannot be explained mechanically or in bodily terms, he said, and so it 'establishes the other part of my theory [for] we are obliged to admit an *indivisible substance* in ourselves, which must itself be the source of its phenomena' (WF 113).

The idea that all bodily events have bodily causes, and mental events mental causes, that 'everything occurs in the soul as if there were no body, just as ... everything happens in the body as if there were no soul' (WF 113), is one of the cruces of Leibniz's doctrine. This does not mean, of course, that a mental act of will is not accompanied by the raising of a bodily arm, or that there is no coincidence between pain and the puncturing of our flesh by a needle. God, Leibniz said,

> created the machinery of the world in such a way that, without constantly breaking ... laws of nature ... it happens that the internal springs of bodies are ready of themselves to act appropriately precisely at the moment that the soul has a conforming desire or thought ... [T]hus the union of the soul with the machinery of the body ... is simply a matter of this concomitance, which exhibits the wonderful wisdom of the creator much better than any other hypothesis. (LA 94–5)

Bayle found this idea most implausible. Having in mind not just natural events, but all the actions and interactions of ourselves and others, it seemed to him just not credible that *everything* in the material world could be a result of purely mechanical material causes. Leibniz, however, was unmoved by this reaction, and made bold claims about the possibilities of mechanism. Just as *we* could make a machine which was 'capable of walking around a town for a time, and of turning precisely at the corners of certain streets' (WF 108), so someone cleverer than a man but still of finite intelligence not only 'could make a ship capable of getting itself to a certain port, by first giving it the route, the direction, and the requisite equipment, but ... could also build a body capable of simulating a man' (WF 109). So, he argued, given the infinite power and wisdom of God the creator, it is not impossible in principle that all bodies in the material world, including our own, are 'natural mechanisms which never go wrong' (WF 110).

The suggestion that our bodies are automata, constructed in such a way as to anticipate our desires and wishes, and that our voluntary actions are a matter, not of mind/body causation, but of a pre-established harmony between our wills and independently caused movements of our bodies, was only one half of what Bayle found hard to accept. He also had problems with Leibniz's claim that rational minds and animal souls too brought about all of their own changes, and were not directly affected by the body. Why, Bayle asked, should minds ever 'give themselves' feelings of pain? Why should a contented dog ever feel pain?

In one way, of course, these questions have an easy answer. The 'pre-established harmony' or 'concomitance' means that minds give themselves pain only because needles are stuck in bodies. The dog ceases to be contented and to feel pain only when its body is hit with a stick. Nevertheless there is still something understandable in Bayle's reaction. According to Leibniz his doctrine of pre-established harmony provides a solution to the problem of the nature of the union between the mind and the body. But in suggesting that the relation between body and mind is one of *non-causal* 'concomitance', or 'correspondence' it might seem that Leibniz was effectively *dis*uniting the mind and the body. There are, however, two features of the pre-established harmony which need to be stressed, for they are supportive of a close union.

The relation of 'agreement', 'harmony' or 'concomitance' between two events, one in the mind and one in the body, involves something more than just that the events are contemporaneous. My pain might be contemporaneous not only with the pricking of my hand with a pin, but also with various digestive activities in my stomach; for, after all, Leibniz holds that the mind, in its perceiving, represents everything in the body. So what relates my pain to the puncturing of my skin rather than to the process of digestion in my stomach? What is there beyond their coinciding that relates the rising of my arm rather than my digestive activities to my desire to move my arm?

The answer lies in the fact that Leibniz's non-causal relation of 'agreement' involves as a further feature a relation of 'mutual expression' or representation between mind and body. In the one direction it is, Leibniz said, the very 'nature of the soul ... to represent the body' (AG 173); and, in the other direction, everything in a person's mind is 'also represented in his body' (WF 112). This 'mutual expression' was touched on in Chapter 5, and the fact that it holds between mind and body was, for Leibniz, a crucial part of their union. Indeed he said that without it pre-established harmony 'would not obtain' (NE 77).

So, Leibniz held, there is a harmony between my pain and my skin being punctured, and not between it and my digestive activities, in that the pain is a 'representation' or 'expression' of the puncturing, and not of the digesting. There is, Leibniz held, a kind of resemblance, a natural structural relationship of expression, between my pain and the rupturing of the skin, in a way there is not between the pain and the digesting. In explaining this Leibniz says that while the round shape of a coin is not naturally represented by the idea of a square, it is represented by that of an ellipse. An ellipse 'represents' or 'expresses' a circle in that for each point on the one there corresponds a point on the other; 'there is a constant and regular relation between what can be said about the one and said about the other' (LA 112). So, in the case of the pinprick, it is certainly true, said Leibniz, that 'pain does not resemble the movement of a pin', but it does, he claimed, 'thoroughly resemble the motions which the pin causes in our body, and [so] might represent them in the soul' (NE 131–2). This idea is intuitively very plausible in the case of the mind's being expressed by the body. It is very easy to think of the movement of my hand as an 'expression' or 'representation' of a desire to move it.

An important point about Leibniz's relation of mutual mind/ body expression or representation is that the pain is supposed not only to represent the parting of the flesh, but also to be represented by it. Similarly the raising of the arm is supposed not only to be represented by the mental desire, but also to represent it. It thus contrasts with the causal relation which Descartes supposes between body and mind, which is not a symmetrical one in this way. That is to say, when an event in the mind (pain, say) is caused by an event in the body (the rupturing of the skin of the arm) the mental event does not cause the bodily event. Similarly, when a bodily event (say, the voluntary movement of a hand) is caused by a mental event (say, the desire to move the hand) the bodily event does not cause the mental one. This means that Descartes is easily able to maintain a distinction between cases where we are passive, as when we feel pain, and cases where we are active, as when we will our arms to rise. Leibniz's relation of mutual expression, on the other hand, does not provide the resources to make such a distinction. As we have seen in Chapter 5, however, Leibniz was able to deal with it in terms of an increase or decrease in perceptual distinctness. Our active willing to raise our arm involves a move to clearer, more distinct, perception; in contrast, our passive feeling of pain involves a change to a state of more confused perception. '[T]hat whose expression is the more distinct is judged to act, and that whose expression is the more confused is judged to be passive' (PM 79).

The second feature of the pre-established harmony which needs to be stressed as being supportive of a close union between body and mind can be brought out by first looking again at Descartes' interactionism. On Descartes' account of it, the union between body and mind is a matter of some events in my corporeal body (such as my arm's rising) having their efficient cause (via the pineal gland) in my mind, and of some mental events (such as my feeling pain) having their cause (again via the pineal gland) in my corporeal body. So the union, according to Descartes, is an intermittent one. This is equally so in the case of occasionalism (with 'occasional' causality replacing 'real' causality). In the case of both interactionism and occasionalism the 'union' is not so close or intimate that *all* events in my body have mental causes, or that *all* mental events have causes in my body. Many events have causes of their own kind.

In his work the *Passions of the Soul* Descartes explained this in some detail. The 'union' between body and mind is intermittent, not complete and thoroughgoing. Many events in the corporeal world have their cause there: many of the functions of human bodies (digestion, commonly accepted as an involuntary activity would be an example) have purely mechanical explanations. Similarly, many mental events have mental causes: many of our 'thoughts' 'proceed directly from our soul … depend on it alone … [and] terminate in the soul itself' (CSM 1.335). So some bodily events have bodily causes and have no mental effects, and some mental events have mental causes and have no bodily effects. In these cases there is *no* connection between the mind and the body. To an extent, the mind and the body lead independent lives.

On the other hand, of course, their lives are not completely independent; there is 'union' between mind and body. Some bodily events *do* have mental causes. Sometimes, that is, thoughts 'proceeding directly from our soul' (CSM 1.335) have an effect beyond the soul or mind, and 'consist of actions which terminate in our body, as when our merely willing to walk has the consequence that our legs move and we walk' (CSM 1.335). Similarly, some mental events have causes in the body or the wider corporeal world: some 'thoughts' proceed neither directly nor indirectly from the soul as their cause, but from the material world. In such cases it is 'not our soul which makes them such as they are, and the soul always receives them from the things that are represented by them' (CSM 1.335) – whether this be our body, as with pain, or 'objects outside us' (CSM 1.337), as with the light of a torch.

Now though Leibniz replaces this intermittent causal interaction (be it 'real', or 'occasional' and mediated *via* God) with a non-causal relation, the 'correspondence', 'harmony' or 'concomitance' between body and mind is complete and not intermittent. Leibniz does not think, as do Descartes and Malebranche, that the 'union' is a matter of *some* bodily (or mental) events being related to mental (or bodily) events. Involved in his theory of harmonious correspondence between body and mind is that they *all* are. '[C]ertain movements, which are rightly called involuntary, have been attributed to the body', by Descartes and the Cartesians, 'to such an extent that they have been believed to have nothing corresponding to them in the soul'. '[C]onversely it has been thought', Leibniz reminds us, 'that certain abstract thoughts are not represented in the body'. 'But both of these', he says, 'are mistaken' (WF 117).

So it is Leibniz's hypothesis that 'to every movement of our body there correspond certain, more or less confused, perceptions or thoughts of our soul' (LA 112–13). The idea that involuntary bodily functions such as digestion have no mental correlate is wrong: 'I even maintain that something happens in the soul corresponding ... to every internal movement of the viscera' (NE 116). Similarly, and in the other direction, 'the body is so constructed that the soul never makes decisions to which bodily movements don't correspond' (WF 112). 'Everything that ambition or whatever other passion produces in Caesar's soul is also represented in his body' (WF 112).

Leibniz said on more than one occasion that the pre-established harmony between mind and body is what constitutes the union between the two. 'The union of soul and body ... consists only in that perfect mutual harmony deliberately set up at the creation, by virtue of which each substance acting according to its own laws is in step with the requirements of the others' (LA 136). 'It is this mutual agreement, arranged in advance in each substance in the universe, which produces what we call their communication, and which alone constitutes *the union of soul and body*' (NS 14). But towards the end of his life, initially in response to an objection by Joseph de Tournemine, he seems to hold that this is insufficient. Tournemine said that '*correspondence*, or *harmony*, does not make a *union*, or essential connection'. Taking up an analogy Leibniz had once used in explaining the pre-established harmony between mind and body, he continued '[w]hatever parallels we imagine between two clocks, even if the relation between them were perfectly exact, we could never say that these clocks were united just because the movements of the one correspond to the movements of the other with perfect symmetry' (Tournemine 1703: 97, 249). In the pre-established harmony, said Tournemine, '[t]here is, if you like, a perfect correspondence; but there is no real connection', there is no 'genuine union' (Tournemine 1703: 248–9).

In response to this Leibniz appeared to concede that the relation of pre-established harmony did fall short of what he called a real 'metaphysical union' (WF 250) between body and mind. Later, in trying to show to Catholics that his philosophy could accommodate the dogma of transubstantiation, he began to refer to the possibility of there being a *vinculum substantiale*, a 'substantial bond' between the two, some 'unifying substance' or reality over and above monads (L 600). Russell, who was never slow to suspect Leibniz's motives, described this as 'rather the concession of a diplomatist than the creed of a philosopher' (Russell 1900: 152). In varying degrees, other commentators have taken Leibniz more seriously on this matter.

FURTHER READING

Cartesian interactionism and Leibniz's objections to it are discussed further in Garber (1983), Loeb (1981: 126–57), McLaughlin (1993), Sleigh (1990a: 139–46).

For Leibniz and Tournemine, see Adams (1994: 295–9), Rutherford (1995a: 273–6), Woolhouse (2000).

On the *vinculum substantiale* see Adams (1994: 299–307), Broad (1975: 124–30), Rescher (1967: 121–3), Rutherford (1995a: 276–82, 1995b: 154–63).

CHAPTER 9

SPACE

The world as we unreflectingly understand it consists at least partly of material bodies existing in space. No explanation is needed as to how Leibniz's 'corporeal substance realism' (as in Chapter 4) squares with this. Its corporeal substances (or their bodies) quite straightforwardly are positioned in space. It is different, however, in the case of the 'monadic aggregate idealism' (of Chapter 4). According to this, material bodies are *phenomena bene fundata*, appearances presented by an aggregate of monads. At the level of material aggregates such as a flock of sheep, or a marble tile, one thing which frequently and at least partially determines co-membership of the aggregate is spatial proximity. But monads are not positioned in space or related to each other spatially. They do, however, have a 'point of view' from which they perceive the whole universe, in varying degrees of distinctness or confusedness.

One way in which Leibniz has been understood here is as holding that their 'point of view' in effect gives monads a spatial position, a position which is determined by the relative distinctness with which different parts of the universe are perceived (Russell 1900: 147; see Adams 1994: 251–2). But, as Leibniz recognized, distinctness of perception is a function not only of proximity but also of size: representation is distinct 'as regards ... things ... that are either nearest or greatest in relation to each of the monads' (Mon 60). Another way of understanding him is to suppose that his intention is that a monad's 'point of view' is given by the spatial position of its body. As we saw in Chapter 5, a monad perceives the whole universe through its representations of the body which belongs to it. On this account the spatial position of monads is given indirectly by the spatial positions of their bodies.

i. CORRESPONDENCE WITH CLARKE

None of this is mentioned, let alone explained, but is merely presupposed, in a controversial correspondence concerning the nature of space which Leibniz had towards the end of his life with an Englishman, Samuel Clarke. Clarke represented the views of Isaac Newton, and the correspondence deals with space (and time, and the vacuum and atoms) as topics in natural philosophy. As such, it operates on a level which for Leibniz is not the most metaphysic-ally basic. There is no mention of monads, and the idea of material bodies which have a location in space is taken for granted. It had an influence on Kant in his discussion of the nature of space, and it shows Leibniz making use of two fundamental general theses in his philosophy: the principle of sufficient reason and the identity of indiscernibles. We should look at these first.

ii. SUFFICIENT REASON

As we saw in Chapter 5, the principle of sufficient reason is one of two great principles on which all our reasoning is based. The other is the principle of contradiction, which is the grounding for necessary truths, or truths of reason. The principle of sufficient reason, which concerns us here, is the grounding for contingent truths, truths of fact whose opposite is possible. As Leibniz explained, 'there can be no real or existing fact, no true statement, unless there is a sufficient reason, why it should be so' (Mon 32). The French philosopher Louis Couturat, writing at the same time as Russell at the very beginning of the twentieth century, went so far as to say that the whole of *Monadology* is derived from this principle (Couturat 1902: 2).

Leibniz gave a number of different accounts or explanations of this 'sufficient reason' which is the ground for contingent truths. What seems to be his most basic relates to his theory of truth, which we encountered in Chapter 3. Given that all propositions are such that the notion of the predicate is contained in the notion of the subject, it follows, he says, as an immediate corollary that 'nothing happens without a reason' (LA 56). Understood in this way the principle obviously applies to all propositions, necessary and contingent alike. In the latter case, however, Leibniz says that their truth depends on the free choices made by God and created things and that there are always reasons for these choices. Since these are founded on 'what is or seems to be the best of several equally possible things' (DM 13), the principle of sufficient reason is also sometimes described as the principle of the best. It is under the second interpretation (specifically with regard to God's choices) that the principle is wielded in the correspondence with Clarke. Finally, Leibniz also describes the principle as holding that 'there is no effect without a cause' (AG 31).

Leibniz told Clarke that the principle of sufficient reason can be 'justified by bare reason, or *a priori*' (LC 96). But at the same time he also suggests it is supported by empirical induction:

> I have often defied people to allege an instance against that Great principle, to bring any one uncontested example wherein it fails. But they have never done it. ... [I]t succeeds in all the known cases in which it has been made use of ... From whence one may reasonably judge, that it will succeed also in unknown cases. (LC 96)

iii. IDENTITY OF INDISCERNIBLES

The principle of the identity of indiscernibles also figures in Leibniz's discussion with Clarke. According to this, 'it is not possible that there should be two individuals who are exactly similar, or who differ only numerically' (LA 54). 'Two leaves, two eggs, two bodies ... are never completely alike' (WF 106–7). Leibniz says the principle follows from his conception of an individual as something which (as in Chapter 3) has a complete notion. That this is what individual substances are like is a necessary truth; and this would make the identity of indiscernibles (at least in so far as it applies to substances) a necessary truth too.

Leibniz, however, also speaks of it as though it were a contingent truth. In claiming that it follows from the principle of sufficient reason, he says to Clarke that he won't say it is 'absolutely impossible to suppose ... two things perfectly indiscernible' (LC 62), but only that it is contrary to God's wisdom to create two such things.

Consistently with allowing that it is not 'absolutely impossible' that there should be two identicals and hence that the principle is contingently true, Leibniz sometimes appeals to empirical fact to support it. He relates how his friend Princess Sophie once defied a visitor, who thought the principle was surely false, to find two identical leaves. The man 'ran all over the garden a long time to look for some; but it was to no purpose' (LC 36). Even two apparently indistinguishable drops of water will appear different when viewed with a microscope, he said.

iv. SPACE AS ABSOLUTE AND AS RELATIVE

Leibniz uses these two principles in his correspondence with Clarke to attack a view of space which he attributes to Isaac Newton (and to Clarke as his representative). At first he describes them as holding that space is 'a substance, or at least an absolute being' (LC 26). Though Newton did seem to make space into a being when he said that 'by existing ... everywhere, he [God] constitutes ... space' (quoted Garber 1995: 302), Clarke disavowed what Leibniz had attributed to them. Space is not 'a being', he said. It is not that space is God, but rather that it is a 'property', or a 'consequence' of God (LC 31) – a consequence, in fact, of his immensity.

Yet Clarke did not deny the 'absoluteness' of space. This involves the idea that space is prior to things in space. As such, space is, as it were, a container of the things in it. Between two things at a distance from each other there is space. The space occupied by a body is different from the internal space or volume of that body; the body is in space, and could move to another part of it. Without space there could have been no things in space. But without things in space there still could have been space. Moreover, as Leibniz describes this view, 'space is something absolutely uniform; and ... one point of space does not absolutely differ in any respect whatsoever from another point of space' (LC 26).

Leibniz found much to object to in this. For a start, though he agreed that God certainly is standardly characterized by immensity, he could not accept that immensity and space could be the same thing. God's immensity means that he is omnipresent, and so would be present in all spaces. But if God is in space how could space be a property of God? Referring to an Aristotelian doctrine, he commented dryly that '[w]e have often heard that a property is in its subject; but we never heard that a subject is in its property' (LC 68).

More fundamentally, Leibniz rejected the idea that space is 'absolute'. Clarke supposes that spatial location is absolute and given by a body's position in absolute space. Against this, Leibniz argues for what is usually referred to as a 'relational' view, according to which the spatial situation of a body is purely relative, and consists only in its relations to other bodies. Space, he says, is 'merely relative'. Without bodies spatially situated relative to each other, there would be 'no actual space' (LC 90). It is an 'order or relation'; and without related bodies it is 'nothing at all ... but the possibility' of there being bodies placed and spatially related (LC 26). Of course Newtonian space may be said to be something which provides the possibility of objects being placed and related in certain ways. But it is something over and above that possibility, something real in itself, something which would exist in the absence of such related objects. There is, however, no need for such a thing, Leibniz insists. There is no need 'to fancy any absolute reality out of the things whose situation we consider' (LC 69).

Space in itself, space abstracted from and considered apart from any set of bodies which are spatially related is 'ideal' (LC 89). Apart from spatially situated things it is not any 'absolute reality' (LC 69). It is 'an ideal thing; containing a certain order, wherein the mind conceives the application of [spatial] relations' (LC 70). Space, Leibniz says, is an 'order of situations, when they are conceived as being possible' (LC 89).

In following Leibniz's arguments against Newtonian absolute space it is not easy to separate out his appeals to the principle of sufficient reason from those to that of the identity of indiscernibles. The discussion insofar as it concerns space focuses on at least three different examples.

1. The possibility of the world's being created in one place rather than another (LC 20, 27): Leibniz argued that if the Newtonians were right that space is absolute then the world would have to have been created in one region of space, or in another region. But God could have no sufficient reason for choosing one region rather than another, since one region does not differ from another. However, God never makes a choice without reason, so if space were absolute, God would not have created a world. But, as we know, he did. So he cannot have been faced with the choice of creating the world in one region of an absolute space rather than another. Therefore, Leibniz concluded, space is not absolute. On the other hand, if, as he holds, space 'is nothing at all without bodies', the question of *where* the world should be created does not arise (LC 26).

2. The possibility of God moving the world from the place where it was created to another: Clarke suggested that this is a real possibility and argued that it is one which only the view that space is absolute can recognize (LC 32). Leibniz, by appeal to the principles of sufficient reason and of the identity of indiscernibles, denied that it was a real possibility at all. It was, therefore, nothing that his view of space needed to take account of.

3. The possibility that God might have placed bodies in space 'the quite contrary way, for instance, by changing East into West' (LC 26): It is clear that if, as Leibniz holds, 'space is nothing else but [an] order or relation; and is nothing at all without bodies' there are not two distinct possibilities here, 'the one would exactly be the same thing as the other' (LC 26). So, on Leibniz's view, the question of a choice between two alignments is ruled out by the identity of indiscernibles and does not arise. The two alignments are 'absolutely indiscernible; and consequently there is no room to enquire after a reason of the preference of the one to the other' (LC 26). But that is *if* space is as Leibniz holds, and in fact he allows that if space were absolute God would indeed have been faced with two possibilities. But what ultimately rules them out here is the principle of sufficient reason. There could have been no sufficient reason for God to make the choice between them and to opt for one alignment rather than the other. (Hence if space were absolute, he would not have created any world at all. But we know that he did.)

Though Leibniz does not discuss this with Clarke at much length, the placing of bodies 'the quite contrary way ... by changing East into West' is not such a straightforward matter as he seems to think. It deserves more consideration, such as was in effect given later by Kant. He drew attention to what have been called 'incongruent counterparts', such as, for example, a right-handed and a left-handed glove, or (to take a simpler, and two-dimensional case) a pair of right-angled triangles, one facing to the right, the other to the left.

These have relevance for Leibniz's and Clarke's discussion because to replace a right-handed glove with its mate, or the right-facing triangle with the left-facing one, is in effect to place something 'quite the contrary way'. What is significant about them is that the relations between the parts of one member of the pairs are exactly the same as the relations between the parts of the other member. In terms of their internal descriptions, the members of these pairs are identical and indiscernible. Leibniz and Clarke would agree on this. They would agree that considering them purely in themselves and without relating them to any direction or any outside point, there is no difference between the gloves, or between the triangles.

Clarke, however, would add that nevertheless there *is* a difference. If God had decided to create a world consisting of just one glove then, Clarke would have added, he would have been faced with the choice between creating a left-hand glove or a right-hand one. Leibniz's relational view of space, however, commits him to saying that those two possibilities 'do not at all differ from each other'; and on the basis of anything he says about this in his discussion with Clarke, it seems he would have been entirely happy about this commitment.

The commitment has awkward consequences, however. Of course, Leibniz would not be involved in saying of the two gloves of a pair that they *are* identical, that there is no difference in handedness *between* them. But given this he would surely have to allow that if God's initial creation consisted just of a pair of gloves there would be a real possibility of his then deciding to destroy either the left or the right. It is curious, then, that the handedness of the remaining glove would seem to have to disappear once it was on its own.

In responding to what Leibniz said about the above three examples Clarke questioned the truth of the principle of sufficient reason, at least as Leibniz understood it. It is true, he agreed, that in the case of the first example it follows from the absolute view of space that God would have been faced with exactly similar alternatives (creating the world in one place rather than another). But it does not follow, he said, that the principle of sufficient reason would require him to do nothing and to make no choice. The sufficient reason for something, he said, is 'oft-times no other, than the mere will of God' (LC 20). Indeed, he said, if God could not choose and act like this, 'without a predetermining cause' (LC 21), he would be really nothing more than a balance which is physically determined one way rather than another. He would not be an intelligent and free cause, and would have no power of choosing. Leibniz's reaction was that Clarke's idea that God's will could of itself be a sufficient reason amounted to a denial of the principle – which Clarke had said he accepted.

In reply, Clarke made a slight change to his case which strengthened it considerably. It was perfectly acceptable, he argued, to suppose that the mere will of God could be the reason for the universe being created in one place rather than another exactly similar place given that there was good reason to put it anywhere at all in the first place (LC 32). 'There may', he said, 'be very good reason to act, though two or more ways of acting may be completely indifferent' (LC 45).

On the face of it what Clarke says here is very plausible. Surely I may have a good reason for getting up and walking out of a room; the fact that I have no reason to put my left foot or my right foot forward first will not prevent me. Leibniz denies this, however. We never, he says, have 'a sufficient reason to act' when there is 'not also a sufficient reason to act in a certain particular manner ... When there is a sufficient reason to do any particular thing, there is also a sufficient reason to do it in a certain particular manner' (LC 60). He says elsewhere that when we start to walk there are reasons which determine us to set one foot forward rather than the other.

Leibniz also took exception to Clarke's claim that unless God could act without a predetermining cause he would be like a balance, robbed of the power of choosing, and something other than an intelligent and free agent. The question of freedom, however, both divine and human, and its relation to the principle of sufficient reason, is a topic for Chapter 11.

FURTHER READING

Frankel (1986), Hanfling (1981), Parkinson (1965: 62–8), Sleigh (1983) discuss the principle of sufficient reason.

On the principle of the identity of indiscernibles in general, see Frankel (1981), Parkinson (1965: 129–37), Russell (1900: sects. 23–6), Sleigh (1983). For this principle as used in the Leibniz-Clarke correspondence specifically, see Chernoff (1981), Vinci (1974), Wilson (1973).

For more on the Leibniz-Clarke correspondence see Broad (1946), Cook (1979), Hartz and Cover (1988), Winterbourne (1982).

CHAPTER 10

GOD AND OUR RELATION TO HIM

i. GOD AND CREATION

Bertrand Russell thought that 'the weakest part' in Leibniz's philosophy is the use it makes of 'the lazy device of reference to an Omnipotent Creator' (Russell 1900: 172). But, unlike Russell, Leibniz was simply not an atheist (we saw in Chapter 1 how much he was concerned with ecumenical questions of church reunion). It is not so much that his philosophy lazily *makes use of* God, as that to a considerable extent it is *about* him, and about the relation between him and ourselves and the world we live in. Moreover, the 'fairy tale' of the *Monadology* is plainly not just all abstract metaphysics. Towards the end it speaks movingly of matters of piety and practical religion. Without God Leibniz's philosophy would be like Shakespeare's 'Romeo and Juliet' without the young lovers.

As Leibniz sees it, his conception of God is simply '[t]he most commonly accepted notion' (DM 1). It is that God is 'an absolutely perfect being' (DM 1). Such a being is one which has all perfections, and perfections are those 'simple' qualities that are 'positive and absolute' (L 167). A simple quality is one that is not analyzable into other qualities; a positive quality is one which is not merely the negation of another; and an absolute quality is one which involves no limit, and has been taken to the highest degree. 'Being the highest number' is not, Leibniz explains, a perfection; it is in fact a contradiction, for number cannot be taken to the highest degree. In contrast however, greatest knowledge and omnipotence involve no impossibility, Leibniz claims, so power and knowledge are perfections, and God has them to the highest degree and without limit. God is perfectly wise and good, too; he wills and acts in the most perfect way.

God's action importantly consists, of course, in creation. 'In God there is *power*, which is the source of all' (Mon 48), the source of all created substances, material or immaterial. He himself is the supreme immaterial substance, a necessarily existing, uncreated 'spirit'. This distinction between uncreated substance on the one hand, and created substance on the other, between God and his creation, was a feature of philosophical thought in Leibniz's time. It is not a completely sharp distinction, for there is some tension between the ideas of being created and dependent on the one hand, and yet substantial on the other. Thus Descartes was led to say that the definition of substance as 'a thing which exists in such a way as to depend on no other thing for its existence' applies properly only to God and not to anything that he created (CSM 1.210). Similarly, as we have seen in earlier chapters, Leibniz argued that occasionalism, with its claim that there is no activity in the created world, amounts to making the world so dependent on God that it is robbed of all substantiality. His own view, of course, as we have seen, is that substantiality *is* perfectly compatible with dependence on a creator, and that there are many substances other than God.

A traditional question and one of some concern in the seventeenth century was how an immaterial being could create a material world. It was sometimes partly answered by supposing that God merely imposed form on already existing matter. In reflecting on it Locke and Newton both made an interesting connection between the action of the human mind on the body and God's creation of matter: 'God ... created the world solely by the act of will just as we move our bodies by an act of will alone' (Newton quoted Westfall 1971: 340). The suggestion is certainly interesting, but it hardly provides a complete solution, for, as Locke admits, we do not know how our minds move our bodies either. He was, nevertheless, convinced that the idea was along the right lines: explain how we will our bodies to move 'and then the next step will be to understand creation' (Locke 1690: IV.x.19). Of course Leibniz could hardly go along with this idea as it stands for, as we saw in some detail in Chapter 8, he denied that our will does move our body, with which it is only in pre-established harmony. Nevertheless like Locke and Newton he thought some light was thrown on the matter by an analogy with our own case. Though we 'cannot understand in detail' (NE 443), he thought, how creation is effected, he sometimes refers to a traditional doctrine of so-called emanation: God continually produces substances 'by a kind of emanation, as we produce our thoughts' (DM 14). Once God has decided which is the best possible world and so what will best 'manifest His glory', he 'make[s] His thought effective' and creates (DM 14).

As just implied, Leibniz's typical thought about the creation of the world is that God reviews an infinity of possible worlds, possibilities which 'have a claim to existence … in proportion to their perfections' (PNG 10). From these, God, in his wisdom and goodness, identifies and chooses the best; and, finally, through his power, he actualizes or creates it. There are times, however, when Leibniz seems to hold that creation does not depend on God's decision and will, and that it is as though the best possible world brings itself into existence. In an essay which he begins by saying that God 'constructs or makes' (PM 136) the world, he goes on to speak as though the essences of the substances which make up the best possible world in God's mind realize themselves *independently* of his will or decision, or even of his understanding, as to which is the best. There is, he says, 'in things that are possible … a certain need for existence … essence in itself tends towards existence', and this 'need' and 'tendency' is all the more pressing in the things of the best possible world (PM 137). There has been a considerable amount of discussion about this. At first it does indeed sound as though, having won the battle for existence by virtue of its highest degree of perfection, the best possible world is self-creating. On the other hand, perhaps Leibniz is really only giving a metaphorical account of the way in which God is presented with and has to choose and decide between many possible worlds, each of which has some claim to exist. What is meant by the best possible world will be looked at in Chapter 12.

ii. PROOFS OF THE EXISTENCE OF GOD

For the moment we should look at Leibniz's proofs of the existence of God. In the *Monadology* he lists three. Of these, one, which is a version of what is traditionally known as 'the ontological argument', is, he says, 'sufficient for us to know the existence of God a priori'. Another argues from 'the reality of eternal truths'; it is not a traditional argument but is original with Leibniz. The last, which is a form of what is known as a 'cosmological argument' gives an 'a posteriori' proof. Elsewhere, Leibniz proposes a fourth argument, a version of an 'argument from design'.

The *ontological argument* originated with Anselm, and was one on which Descartes relied. In describing it as '*a priori*', he meant that, rather than arguing from some actual effect of God to the existence of God himself as its cause as does an '*a posteriori*' argument, it reflects directly on the very idea of God as a most perfect being. Just as reflection on the idea or essence of a triangle reveals the necessary truth that the three angles must equal two right angles, so in the same way, Descartes said, the idea of a perfect being includes existence. As a result, the conclusion is not merely that God exists, but that, since existence is part of his essence, God necessarily exists. Typically, Leibniz says, the argument runs like this: I have 'an idea of God or of a perfect being ... Now the idea of this Being includes all the perfections, and existence is one of these, so that consequently He exists' (DM 23). As thus typically put, Leibniz thinks, the argument is faulty and needs amendment.

Since Leibniz's time such an argument has been criticized, most notably by Kant, on the grounds that 'existence' cannot be thought of as a perfection. To think of it as such involves thinking of it as a property, like being powerful, or wise. Yet, Kant argued, '[b]y whatever and by however many predicates we may think a thing – even if we completely determine it – we do not make the least addition to the thing when we further declare that this thing *is*' (Kant 1781/1787: A600/B628). In more recent times Kant's point has been captured by the idea that 'exists' is not an ordinary descriptive predicate, but is a second-order predicate, a predicate of predicates. It does not form part of a description, but says *of* a description, that something exists which answers to it. But Leibniz had no objection to the argument on this score. He agreed with his near contemporaries Descartes and Spinoza that 'existence' is 'a predicate' that might form part of the description of something, so that 'tame tigers exist' is logically on a par with 'tame tigers growl'. He agreed, too, that 'existence' is a perfection and as such is contained in and can be derived from the idea of God, the perfect being.

The fault with the argument, Leibniz argued, is that it is incomplete and needs supplementation. What it proves is not so much that 'God, the perfect being, exists' as that '*if the most perfect being, God, is possible* then God exists'. As typically stated, the argument assumes without any proof that 'the most perfect being does not involve a contradiction' (PM 76).

On the face of it, of course, the idea of the most perfect being is certainly not obviously incoherent – as the idea of a square circle obviously is. But this is not sufficient, Leibniz says. He makes the interesting point that we can think of things which are possible on the face of it, but which on closer investigation prove not to be. An example he gives of such 'impossible chimerae' (DM 23) is that of a regular solid figure with ten equal sides, a regular decahedron. A solid figure with six equal faces is perfectly possible, so why not one of ten? It can be shown, however, that within Euclidian geometry such a figure is not possible.

Fortunately for the ontological argument, it is not too difficult, Leibniz thought, to supplement it in the required way. It is not difficult to show that the idea of a perfect being is perfectly coherent, and that God is possible. '[N]othing can interfere with the possibility of that which involves no limits, no negation and consequently no contradiction' (Mon 45). Perfections, which all of God's properties are, are, we have seen, simple and positive. They are all properties which are unanalyzable and not formed by the negation of some other property. As such they are mutually compatible, and so a being which was characterized by them all is perfectly possible. The only way, Leibniz argues, that *some hidden* incompatibility could be shown would be by analyzing them, but since they are simple they have no analysis.

One criticism of Leibniz's proof of the possibility of a perfect being is that it seems to allow us to prove the necessary existence of less than perfect beings too (see Adams 1994: 151). Given his claim that simple positive properties cannot be inconsistent, it follows that there can be no inconsistency between a number of simple positive properties and the negation of another simple positive property. So the idea of a being which lacks one perfection (say goodness), but has all the others including existence, is perfectly coherent. Hence, given the principle of the ontological argument, it follows that such a being necessarily exists.

Leibniz's argument for the existence of God from '*the reality of eternal truths*' is not a version of a traditional argument. Some of its ideas are not new, but there is innovation in his applying them to a demonstration of God. Unfortunately for its reputation Russell described the argument as 'scandalous' (Russell 1900: 178); Broad, however, was 'pretty sure' that Russell had 'completely misunderstood' it (Broad 1975: 157), and more recently Adams has said it 'deserves attention', and is 'more persuasive' than any version of the ontological argument (Adams 1994: 177). It will be useful to set Leibniz's argument against the background of Descartes.

In discussing the truths of mathematics and geometry, paradigm examples of what were variously called necessary, eternal or essential truths, Descartes said that, *like everything else*, they 'depend on' God (K 11). The dependency that he had in mind is rather surprising. He believed that they depended on God's *will*, in that they depend *for their truth* on some divine decision. God 'laid down these laws in nature, just as a king lays down laws' (K 11). It is easy to see that someone might say this of contingent truths, whose opposite is entirely possible. It is easy to see that someone might hold that it was by some decision and act of will on God's part that, for example, some areas of the world suffer from earthquakes. But Descartes says this of necessary truths too. He claims that '[j]ust as He [God] was free not to create the world, so He was no less free to make it untrue that all the lines drawn from the centre of a circle to its circumference are equal' (K 11). Descartes does not mean to say that necessary truths are not necessarily true and are no different from contingent truths. He is not abandoning the traditional view that geometrical truths are not merely contingently true empirical generalizations, but are essentially true, true by virtue of the essences of geometrical figures. His claim is, rather, that these essences themselves are dependent on God's will and might have been different. He did not will that the essence of the circle was such that circles had unequal radii, but he could have done so.

At first sight it might seem that Leibniz was in agreement with Descartes. He held not only that geometrical truths are true essentially, true by virtue of certain essences, but also that these essences depend on God. God, he said 'is not only the source of existences, but also that of essences' (Mon 43). Leibniz differed from Descartes, however, in holding that necessary or eternal truths and the essences they derive from do not depend on God's *will*. They are entirely independent of that. What they depend on is God's *understanding*: we should not think that 'the eternal truths, being dependent on God, are arbitrary and depend on his will, as Descartes held ... [T]hey depend solely on his understanding' (Mon 46). So, Leibniz holds, God's understanding is 'the region of eternal truths or of the ideas on which they depend' (Mon 43); God is the source 'of what is real in the possible'; without God 'not only would there be nothing existing but nothing would even be possible' (Mon 43). Contingent truths too, truths about what is *actually* the case in the created world, depend on God's understanding (as to what world is the best possible); but they depend on his will too, on his decision to create the best. Essential truths however, truths which are true by virtue of essences, truths about what is *necessary* or *possible*, depend only on God's understanding. So, Leibniz holds, the divine understanding is the source of 'that which is real in such truths'. Without God's understanding, Leibniz's view is, there would be no essential truths, such as those of geometry and mathematics. This does not mean that the truths of geometry would be other than what they are; it means, rather, that there would be no truths of geometry at all. At least, there would be no such thing as geometry understood, as it usually is, as an *a priori* non-empirical science, a body of necessary truths. Leibniz's argument is in effect that since eternal truths could not exist unless they subsisted in God's mind, and since there are eternal truths, such as those of geometry and mathematics, then God (or at least an eternal mind) must exist. Leibniz stresses that of course 'it is true that an atheist may be a geometrician'; his point is that 'if there were no God geometry would have no object' (T 243). Without God's understanding for the relevant essences to subsist in there would, so Leibniz's thought is, be no essences, and hence no eternal truths, no arithmetic or geometry.

Without considering in detail how Leibniz might reply to them we should at least note some possible responses to his argument. One, echoing Thomas Hobbes, simply denies the very idea of eternal truth, and rejects Leibniz's assertion that there is 'reality in essences or possibilities, or rather in eternal truths' (Mon 44). So-called 'essential truths', it might be said, are really just a matter of verbal definition. As the logical positivists of the last century held, '[t]hey simply record our determination to use words in a certain fashion' (Ayer 1936: 84). Accordingly, geometry would not be a body of 'essential' or 'eternal' truths, but rather a collection of definitions or consequences drawn from them. Another response, following John Stuart Mill in the nineteenth century, would suggest that supposedly essential or eternal truths are simply very well established empirical generalizations; geometrical truths are contingent truths based on such a large number of confirming observations that we take them to be necessarily true. However, an underlying and *prima facie* entirely plausible premise of Leibniz's second argument for the existence of God is that geometry *does* exist as a body of *a priori* necessary truth, and neither of these two responses does justice to that thought. In favour of his argument is the fact that it acknowledges that *a priori* status, and embodies an answer to the question of what geometrical and mathematical truths depend on for their necessary truth.

Unlike the ontological argument, the third argument for God which Leibniz listed is one which proves his existence in an '*a posteriori*' fashion. That is to say, it argues from an effect of God, back to the cause of that effect, God himself. In this case it takes as a premise the existence of the ordered universe or cosmos (hence the description of it as 'cosmological'), and argues back to a creator. In presenting it, Leibniz depends on the principle of sufficient reason, one of his fundamental principles, which we encountered in Chapters 5 and 9. Appealing to it here, Leibniz argues that though any particular fact in the world is explicable by reference to some other prior particular, this could 'proceed into endless detail', and so we 'are no further ahead' (Mon 36). His argument is not, however, that there must, after all, be some beginning to this backward series, some first cause. It is, rather, that *outside of* this endless series of contingencies which constitutes the world as a whole, there must be a 'sufficient or final reason' (Mon 37).

This 'final reason' must be a necessarily existing being and it is, says Leibniz, what we call 'God'. Even if we do call it 'God', however, it must be acknowledged that at most the argument shows is that there must be something which is responsible for the existence of the world, namely a creator. Even if it were granted that such a creator would have to be omnipotent, that is still some way from its being the possessor of all perfections, the God whose existence Leibniz really aims at proving.

Leibniz proposes a fourth argument for the existence of God. It is surprising that he does not list it in the *Monadology* along with the others, for at one point he says that is one of the strongest arguments he has at his disposal. What he presents is a form of what used to be called the physico-theological argument, more commonly known now as the argument from design. Unlike the cosmological argument, which argues from the existence of the world as a whole, it begins from particular features of the world, features which, it is argued, imply a designer. Perhaps the most famous proponent of such an argument has been William Paley (1743–1805). We would never suppose of a watch we came across that it had been formed by natural forces. It would seem clearly designed and made for a purpose. 'The inference ... is inevitable', says Paley, 'there must have existed, at some time or other, an artificer or artificers who formed it for the purpose which we find it actually to answer, who completely comprehended its construction and designed its use' (Paley 1802: ch. 1). Yet the living organisms and their parts which we come across in nature are more complicated still, 'in a degree which exceeds all computation' (Paley 1802: ch. 3). They too must have had an intelligent designer.

In his 'argument from design' Leibniz might well have appealed to the kind of physical detail in the world to which Paley appealed. We will see in Chapter 12 when we look at what he has in mind in supposing that this world is the 'best possible' that such detail was something which impressed him. In fact he appealed to a feature of the world which was, so to speak, dreamt of only in his own idiosyncratic philosophy. In the pre-established harmony (as in Chapters 7 and 8) between the substances of the world he finds what he says is 'a new and surprisingly clear proof of the existence of God'. '[T]his perfect agreement of so many substances which have no communication with one another could come only from their common cause' (NS 119–20). Without God, he argues, such intricate and extensive harmony would be too much of a coincidence.

iii. GOD AND HIS RELATION TO THE CREATED WORLD

Besides being, generally speaking, its creator, God is related to the world in two different and more specific ways. As in the 'fairy tale' of Chapter 2, he is related to it as an architect, a designer or as 'an inventor is to his machine'; and he is related to it as a monarch or a moral legislator, as 'a prince is to his subjects' or as 'a father is to his children' (Mon 84). Leibniz describes the world under the first of these aspects as the 'Kingdom of Nature'. This is the world as the 'mechanical philosophy' sees it, the physical world regulated by efficient causality and by the laws of motion. But within this natural world there is an order of things which constitutes what Leibniz calls the 'Kingdom of Grace', or the 'City of God'. This specifically human order is a 'moral world', a world regulated not by mechanical laws, but by an awareness of and desire for the good.

All created substances are members of the Kingdom of Nature. We have seen that all substances reflect, in varying degrees of distinctness, the whole world. Their bodies, with which their souls are in pre-established harmony, react to all physical changes in the universe. In doing so they are fulfilling the basic function or purpose of all substances, the reason for which they were created in the first place, to be 'living mirrors or images' of God's creation, the world understood as the Kingdom of Nature (Mon 83). We have seen (Chapter 5), however, that there are differences between substances according to the level and nature of their mental activity. At the top of the hierarchy are rational minds. The possession of such minds gives humans not only the ability to reason, but also a moral identity. This means that humans express not just, as any substance does, God's Kingdom of Nature, but also God himself. Humans are not only 'mirror[s] of ... created things', but also 'image[s] of the Deity' (PNG 14). This makes them members of the Kingdom of Grace and of the City of God.

There are different aspects to being an 'image of the Deity'. Related to the fact that humans have an ability to reason is that we are able to create something which resembles what he created. Besides being mirrors of what God created, reflecting the world through its relation to our bodies, we are therefore mirrors of the creator too. One thing Leibniz has in mind here is that we can *understand* the created world, as well as just reflecting it. We are able, as natural philosophers, to investigate and discover the laws which govern the Kingdom of Nature. Leibniz also has in mind the fact that, as mathematicians and geometers, we can come to know the 'eternal' truths which reside in God's understanding.

Besides having the ability to reason and to 'mirror the creator' in these ways, humans are moral beings too, with a moral identity. They mirror their creator also in being aware of God, able to know and admire his greatness and goodness and in a position to love him. As members of the Kingdom of Grace they are able, like God himself, but unlike things subject to the purely mechanical causality of the Kingdom of Nature, to act voluntarily, according to final causes – according to their perception of what is right and good.

Because of this and because, as rational souls, human beings have self-consciousness and memory, they are susceptible to divine reward and punishment. Indeed, Leibniz assures us that in the Kingdom of Grace no crime goes unpunished, no good action unrewarded. Exactly what he has in mind here is not clear. There is some suggestion of a Judgement Day, in a reference to 'the great future' (PNG 16). He also refers to the destruction and restoration of the earth 'when the government of spirits requires it, for the punishment of some and the reward of others' (Mon 88). This destruction is said to take place 'by natural means' (Mon 88), but it is not obvious that Leibniz has in mind anything so dramatic as some day of final reward and retribution when, speaking of a harmony between the kingdoms of grace and of nature, he says that 'sins must carry their penalty with them, through the order of nature, and even in virtue of the mechanical structure of things' (Mon 89). Conceivably he has in mind that an intemperate life tends naturally (though not inevitably) to unhappy pains of ill health, but what he means is not spelt out.

FURTHER READING

God and Creation

Concerning Leibniz's apparent suggestion that the best possible world creates itself Blumenfeld (1973) argues for a literal reading, Wilson (1989: 275–81) for a metaphorical one.

Proofs of the Existence of God

Broad (1975: ch. 7.2), Parkinson (1965: 76–103), Rescher (1979: ch. 14), Russell (1900: ch. 15) provide discussion of all the proofs. For the onto-logical argument in particular, see Adams (1994: chs. 5–6), Blumenfeld (1972, 1995a), Gotterbarn (1976), Lomansky (1970); for the argument from eternal truths, see Adams (1994: ch. 7), Broad (1975: ch. 7.2.4), Russell (1900: sects. 111–13); and for the cosmological argument, see Blumenfeld (1995a).

God and his Relation to the Created World

For further discussion of the harmony between the kingdoms of nature and of grace, see Bennett (2005), Brown (1988), Hirschmann (1988), Ruther-ford (1995a, chs. 1–3), Savile (2000: ch. 10).

CHAPTER 11

CONTINGENCY AND FREEDOM

i. HUMAN FREEDOM

A perennial criticism of Leibniz's philosophy is that it cannot accommodate freedom. Indeed, it was just this issue that immediately disturbed Arnauld when he read the summary of the *Discourse on Metaphysics*, which Leibniz had sent him. Faced with Leibniz's claim that each person's individual notion 'includes once and for all everything that will ever happen to him' (DM 13), Arnauld drew the conclusion that everything that happened to Adam must have done so through a 'fatal necessity'. Leibniz seems to have satisfied Arnauld in the end. But the question of the compatibility of his metaphysics with human freedom in particular, and contingency in general, is one which Leibniz was made to face by others of his contemporaries and has been raised by his readers ever since. On the whole they have not been satisfied.

In fact the issue makes itself felt beyond Leibniz's doctrine of the completeness of substances. As he himself said quite early on, '[o]ne of the oldest doubts of mankind concerns the question of how freedom and contingency are compatible with the chain of causes' (L 263). One solution to this doubt would be to claim that, whatever the case in the purely material world, our minds, specifically our decisions and will, are not subject to a chain of causes. But Leibniz would have nothing to do with such a solution. For as we have seen in Chapters 9 and 10, one of his fundamental tenets is the principle of sufficient reason according to which 'a reason can be given for every truth, or as is commonly said, that nothing happens without a cause' (PM 75). There is no obvious problem in supposing that this principle holds true of the physical world of material bodies. Potentially more problematically, however, Leibniz was in no doubt that it was true of our minds too. It would be a mistake, he said, to think that 'the great principle which states that nothing comes to pass without cause only related to the body', for the soul is no more capable than the body of 'acting without being determined by some reason or cause' (T 321). So, just as much as the movements of a material body, our decisions and our will are determined by a sequence of causes. Our will is determined 'by the dispositions of the particular immediate cause, which lie in the inclinations of the soul' (T 344). 'The sequence of causes', he said, 'always contributes to the determination of the will' (T 147).

But though Leibniz held that determinism reigned in both body and mind alike, he did not think this meant that we are not free. Determinism and liberty are absolutely compatible; 'free' must not be confused with 'indifferent'; 'free' and 'determined' are not antitheses. The fact that there are always reasons that make us act affects neither our spontaneity nor our freedom.

Yet Leibniz's view was not just that freedom and determinism are compatible; it was, more strongly, that the first does not exist without the second. This is something that came out in his correspondence with Clarke when he rejected (as in Chapter 9) Clarke's suggestion that God's will might of itself be a sufficient reason for his acting. If God's choice were not determined by some reason for acting as he does, his action would not be free but indifferent and random.

It is a misconception to suppose that freedom could consist in 'an indetermination or an indifference of equipoise, as if one must needs be inclined equally ... in the direction of different courses, when there are several of them to take' (T 143). And in fact all our experience shows that in making a free choice we are never in reality indifferent. We are 'always more inclined and consequently more determined on one side than on another' (T 203). We may imagine we are sometimes in an 'indifferent' situation and choose arbitrarily, as for example when we get up from a seat and set off on one foot rather than another. But in fact it is simply that we are not aware of what prompts us, in putting one foot before the other (T 143).

Just as it might initially be thought that freedom and determinism are incompatible, so it might be thought that moral accountability and punishment have no place within a deterministic framework. If in eating the apple Adam was 'determined to sin in consequence of certain prevailing inclinations' how can it be appropriate to punish him? (T 346). Leibniz is quite clear that it can be, and indeed that if our future actions were *not* in part determined by our past experiences, praise and blame would be inappropriate; penalties and rewards would have no point 'if they could not contribute towards determining the will to do better another time' (T 347).

So, for Leibniz, being free necessarily involves being determined. But it is not the same as it. There are, he pointed out, many things in nature which are determined, but where the question of freedom does not arise. A ball rolling down a hill is causally determined to do so, but it is not free. So freedom must be more than or different from determination simply as such. In fact, Leibniz held, it consists altogether in three things: 'in intelligence, which involves a clear knowledge of the object of deliberation, in spontaneity, whereby we determine, and in contingency, that is, in the exclusion of logical or metaphysical necessity' (T 303).

In effect these three criteria serve to clarify the determinism of freedom. This is explicit in the case of the second, 'spontaneity', which makes clear that the compatibility of freedom with determination is compatibility not with just any determination but only with determination of a certain kind. Freedom is not, for example, compatible with being constrained or externally forced. 'When we act freely we are not being forced', as we would be if we were pushed over a precipice (T 143). What is required for freedom is that '*we* determine'. Leibniz's criterion of spontaneity, which in fact goes back to Aristotle, spells out that the determination involved in freedom is *self*-determination. In acting freely we are determined, but what determines us, the principle of our action, is internal.

So being 'spontaneous', as Leibniz means it, has nothing to do with acting on the spur of the moment, nor (as we have seen above) acting for no reason. We are spontaneous if we 'have within us the source of our actions' (T 303). The fact of our being causally determined in our actions, the fact that there are chains of causes leading up to them, does not stand in the way of those actions being free, so long as *we* determine them.

Leibniz claimed that there can be no question but that our actions are spontaneous given all that he has said about the self-containedness of substances. All of that 'demonstrates beyond a doubt that ... each substance is the sole cause of all its actions, and that it is free of all physical influence from every other substance. ... [T]his system shows that our spontaneity is real' (T 309). As it stands, however, this is not satisfactory, and if it shows anything about freedom, it shows too much, and too easily. For if it shows that any of our actions (or indeed all those of substances of any kind) are spontaneous and (so far as that goes) free, it shows that they all are. As a consequence it destroys the requisite distinction, with which Leibniz introduced the spontaneity criterion, between acting freely and being forced. Fortunately Leibniz has a defence against this criticism for though in a 'metaphysically rigorous sense' (NE 210) substances are always 'the sole cause of their actions' (as we saw in Chapter 5) he nevertheless is able to draw and sustain a distinction between actions which can be attributed to the substance itself and those which we attribute to an outside cause. Through their appetition substances are subject to continual change and move from one perceptual state to another. Sometimes that change brings a substance 'closer to its own perfection', and in this case the change can, (speaking in a metaphysically relaxed way), be attributed to the substance itself; sometimes the reverse happens and in this case it may be said that substance is passive and subject to external constraint (NE 211).

A second proviso on the determination which is compatible with, or which constitutes, freedom is that it must be mediated *via* a judgement as to what is best. The very 'soul of freedom' is that it consists 'in intelligence, which involves a clear knowledge of the object of deliberation' (T 303). The 'sufficient reasons' that determine our will must involve judgement.

Intelligence involves the ability to deliberate and to make a judgement as to which is the best of different courses of action; and 'when there is no judgement', Leibniz said, 'there is no freedom' (T 143). Brute animals are not free. Their actions are not free, voluntary or willed. They do not have rational souls and cannot deliberate about the best thing to do. '[T]o will is to be brought to act through a reason perceived by the intellect' (L 389). '[E]very act of will presupposes a judgement of the intellect about goodness' (PM 77).

Though, unlike other animals, we can deliberate about what to do, our judgement as to what is best is fallible. We are not perfectly rational and clear in our reasoning. It is often muddled and influenced by our emotions and mood, 'mixed up ... with the impact of base and confused perceptions' (L 389). As a consequence we are not perfectly free. Only God is perfectly free, only his will, Leibniz says, 'always follows the judgements of the understanding' (T 313).

A consequence of the fact that freedom involves a judgement about what is best is that though it is incompatible with metaphysical or logical necessity, it is closely connected with a kind of necessity which Leibniz calls 'moral'. 'Moral necessity' is the obligation that there is on 'the wisest to choose the best' (T 345). But this, he said, does not detract from liberty; on the contrary, it adds to it. 'To be morally compelled by wisdom, to be bound by the consideration of good, is to be free' (T 273).

Sometimes in describing the effect of all these different determinants (rational judgements, emotions, unconscious perceptions) on the will Leibniz uses analogies from mechanics. The force which determines the movement of a body may be a composite of a number of different forces tending to move it in different directions. Similarly, Leibniz says, '[r]easons in the mind of a wise being, and motives in any mind whatsoever, do that which answers to the effect produced by weights in a balance' (LC 55). The reaction of Leibniz's correspondent Samuel Clarke was, as noted in Chapter 9, that this leads to 'universal necessity' (LC 45), the antithesis of freedom. Such a reaction might well be apt if the only things in the balance were (as would be the case with animals) feelings and unconscious perceptions; but it is crucial to Leibniz's position that judgements of a rational intellect go into it too, and we do find it perfectly natural to describe even rational deliberation as a matter of 'weighing' different considerations.

Again in describing the 'sufficient reasons' which determine our wills Leibniz often, and quite famously, says that in making a choice our wills are 'inclined but not necessitated'. 'There is', he said, 'always a prevailing reason which prompts the will to its choice, and for the maintenance of freedom for the will it suffices that this reason should incline without necessitating' (T 148). He adopted this terminology from an astrological belief about the influence the stars are supposed to have on our lives: 'the stars incline, but do not necessitate' (T 147). Now it might be thought that what lies behind this is an attempt to soften his determinism to make it apparently more palatable to those who think that determinism and freedom are not compatible. We should, however, resist any temptation to think this. For one thing, Leibniz says that the analogy between the determining influences on our will and the influences which the stars are popularly supposed to have on our lives is less than perfect: while the stars are not believed to determine our lives completely, he holds that our wills are *completely* determined by the sum total of all the influences on them. '[T]he course to which the will is more inclined never fails to be adopted' (T 147). So there is certainly no softening or toning down of his determinism. The contrast Leibniz is making between 'inclination' and 'necessity' is not between partial and complete determination. Rather it is between determination and logical or metaphysical necessity. In reminding us that 'free' and 'determined' are not opposed to each other, and that though one is always 'inclined and consequently ... determined' one is 'never necessitated to the choice that one makes', he adds 'I mean here a *necessity* absolute and metaphysical' (T 203). His point is that being determined by our judgement as to what is the best, and by all the other things which, in our imperfect freedom, influence us, is not the same as being absolutely, logically or metaphysically, necessitated.

Not only is being determined not the same as being metaphysically necessitated, it is completely incompatible with it. The *absence* of absolute, metaphysical necessity is the last of the three elements Leibniz finds in freedom. Freedom consists in part, he said, 'in contingency, that is, in the exclusion of logical or metaphysical necessity' (T 303). Metaphysical necessity rules out the possibility of any alternative, and where there are no alternatives about which to deliberate and choose there can be no question of our being free. For a bachelor, while remaining a bachelor, there is no alternative but to be unmarried.

The contingency criterion of freedom is one which caused Leibniz most difficulty. There was no question about its actually being a criterion that an act could not be said to be free if it were logically or metaphysically necessary. The problem was how, within his philosophy, he could show that it was ever actually satisfied. Given that each person's notion involves everything that will ever happen to them then, as Arnauld urged, does it not follow that everything that happened to Adam must have been 'fatally necessary' (DM 13)? Leibniz did not need this pointing out. In the main body of the *Discourse on Metaphysics*, which Arnauld had not been sent, he himself acknowledged that there was indeed 'a great difficulty' here. On the face of it, it did seem that his claim about complete individual substances meant that 'the difference between necessary and contingent truths will be destroyed ... there will no longer be any room for human liberty, and absolute fate will reign over all our actions as well as over all other events in the world' (DM 13).

At various times, in various different ways, and with varying degrees of success, Leibniz faced this difficulty. It is perhaps worth spelling it out by first dwelling on this distinction between contingent and necessary or essential truths, between truths whose opposite is logically or metaphysically possible and those whose opposite is impossible. The distinction, broadly speaking, was generally accepted in Leibniz's time, as it is today. Arnauld gave a good, informal account of it which fits our intuitions. By 'consulting', as he says, the relevant notions or ideas, we can come to see that a circle is such that all the points on its circumference are equidistant from its centre. So, it is indeed natural to say that it is contained in the notion or essence of a circle that circles are like this. A figure would not be a circle if it did not have this property. It is necessarily true that circles are like this. On the other hand if one thinks of what it is to be Arnauld, it seems plain that though he in fact had no children, there is no impossibility in saying that he could have been a father. 'Being childless' does not seem to be contained in the notion of Arnauld, for it is simply contingently true that he was. So the 'great difficulty' facing Leibniz stems from his claim that everything which happens to a person *is* included in his notion, 'just as we can see in the nature of the circle all the properties that can be derived from it' (DM 13). It seems to rule out contingent truths and make all truth necessary.

One explanation of how contingent truths can still be admitted which is often attributed to Leibniz goes like this. Since everything that happens to a person is included in their nature or notion it has to be admitted, so the explanation accepts, as necessarily true that if Elizabeth I exists then she dies a spinster. But it does not follow that it is necessarily true that Elizabeth I dies a spinster. Why not? Because it is not necessarily true that Elizabeth I existed. In fact she did, and so of course she died a spinster. But it is merely contingently true that she existed. God could have created a different world, one in which she did not exist. Existence is not part of the concept of any actual or possible created substance. So it is only contingently true that Elizabeth died a spinster.

Arnauld would not have been satisfied with this. He accepted that God might not have created this world and hence that it was contingent that Elizabeth I existed. But his worry was: given that it was necessarily true that if God created Elizabeth I he would have created a woman who died a spinster, then in creating Elizabeth I, he had no choice but to create a woman who died a spinster. This was parallel, as Arnauld saw it, to saying that if God created a human being then he had no choice but to create a being capable of thought, or to saying that if God created a spinster then he had no choice but to create an unmarried woman. Arnauld said that if this is not what Leibniz thought then he just did not understand what he meant when he said that 'the individual notion of each person involves once for all all that will ever happen to him' (LA 27).

In reply, Leibniz said that Arnauld was wrong in supposing that he thought that it was necessarily true that if God created Elizabeth I he would have created a lifelong spinster. He did not think, Leibniz said, that it is necessarily true that Elizabeth I was a lifelong spinster; he did not think that the truth that she was is on a par with the undoubtedly necessary truth that a spinster is an unmarried woman.

It was, he agreed, quite *certain* at Elizabeth's birth that she would die unmarried. Given the principle of sufficient reason it was determined at her birth that she would die unmarried. But its being certain and determined that she would is not the same as its being metaphysically necessary that she would. There is a difference, Leibniz said, between the proposition that if any woman is a spinster then she is unmarried, and the proposition that if Elizabeth I existed she would die a spinster. Arnauld, of course, did not disagree with this: clearly there is a difference, the first is necessary, the second is contingent. The problem was that he just did not see how Leibniz could maintain this.

In explanation Leibniz said that 'the connection or derivation is of two kinds' (DM 13). The connection between being a spinster and being an unmarried woman is of a different kind from that between being Elizabeth I and being unmarried. The connection in the first case is 'absolutely necessary (its contrary implies a contradiction)'; the connection in the other 'in itself is contingent, since its contrary does not imply a contradiction' (DM 13). In different places, and at different times, Leibniz gives different accounts of these two kinds of connection.

In immediate reply to Arnauld Leibniz insisted that there was a difference between incomplete or 'abstract notions' of species or kinds of thing (such as, e.g., 'spinster', 'king', 'human being' or geometrical concepts such as that of a circle), and the 'notions of individual substances' (such as that of Julius Caesar or Elizabeth I). Notions of the first kind 'contain only necessary or eternal truths'; ones of the second kind 'contain contingent truths or truths of fact' (LA 49).

Is Leibniz claiming here that there are different ways (necessarily, or accidentally and contingently) in which something might be contained in a concept? Or is he claiming that that there are different things (necessities, contingencies) that might be contained in a concept? If he is claiming the first, as on the face of it he is, then he would be saying, rather oddly and evasively, that Caesar was indeed necessitated to cross the Rubicon (because to do so was part of his concept) but that what he was necessitated to do was contingently contained in his concept. Perhaps, then, we should be more generous and take him to be stressing that there surely is a difference between the two kinds of concept. This, again, is not something with which Arnauld would disagree. But what he needed from Leibniz was some explanation of what underlies or accounts for the difference.

Fortunately Leibniz did say something more. The first kind of connection, he said, is founded on 'absolutely pure ideas and God's bare understanding alone', the second is founded also on God's 'free decrees' (DM 13). Contained in the notions of individual substances, considered as possible, are 'God's free decisions (also considered as possible), because those free decisions are the principal source of existences or facts; whereas essences are in the divine understanding before consideration by the will' (LA 49). '[P]ossibles are possible before any of God's actual decisions, but not without presupposing those same decisions considered as possible' (LA 51).

In the light of Leibniz's further explanation of this his thinking seems to be that just as the actual world embodies certain laws of nature (certain laws of motion for example), so do possible worlds, and the laws they embody may be different from case to case. So a certain substance is possible in a given world, not merely relative to metaphysical necessities, but also relative to the laws of nature that apply in it, the choice and actualization of which would depend on a free decision of God.

Though there are hints of it in the *Discourse on Metaphysics* and the ensuing correspondence with Arnauld, Leibniz elsewhere spells out a different account of his claim that the concept of the subject and the concept of the predicate are differently related in necessary and contingent propositions. In the case of necessary truths it is possible 'through an analysis of terms' (AG 28) to demonstrate that the predicate is contained in the subject. But in the case of contingent propositions the analysis 'continues ... to infinity ... so that one never has a complete demonstration ... but [the] reason for the truth ... is understood completely only by God, who alone traverses the infinite series in one stroke of mind' (AG 28). He illustrates this by suggesting that the difference between the way in which predicates are contained in the subjects of necessarily true and contingently true propositions is like the difference between commensurable and incommensurable quantities.

What, first of all, are commensurable and incommensurable quantities? Two sides of a rectangle are (it can be proved) always commensurable: that is to say the ratio between them will always be a whole number or a finite (or a recurring) decimal. (In a 4 by 3 rectangle, for example, the ratio of two sides is 3/4 or .75.) There may also be commensurability between a side of a rectangle and its diagonal. (The diagonal of a 4 by 3 rectangle, for example, is 5; and so the ratio between it and one of the sides is 5/4 or 1.25.) With a square, however, there is no commensurability between sides and diagonal. (The diagonal of a 1 by 1 square is the square root of 2; and the square root of 2 – it can be proved – is an infinite non-recurring decimal, known as a surd.)

It is possible, therefore, to work out exactly how 4 is contained in 3, but there is no finite answer to the division of the square root of 2 by 1. Relating this to the two different ways in which a predicate is contained in a subject, Leibniz's suggestion is that just as it is possible to arrive at a 'common measure' (AG 29) between 4 and 3, and to come to an end in working out how 4 is contained in 3, so 'in necessary propositions ... through a continual analysis of the predicate and the subject, things can at last be brought to the point where it is apparent that the notion of the predicate is in the subject' (AG 28–9). By contrast, the resolution of the 'proportion or relation' between root 2 and 1, the containment of 1 in root 2, 'proceed[s] to infinity and never end[s]' (AG 29), and the parallel here is with contingent truths. In their case 'there *is* a connection between the terms' (AG 29, italics added). The predicate is contained in the subject, but, again, the demonstration of that containment proceeds to infinity and never ends.

From a distance it is easy enough to see something of what Leibniz has in mind here, but it is not easy to apply the comparison in detail. Though we can never finish the calculation, we can work out to some degree of approximation how 1 is contained in the square root of 2. But how are we to begin to work out that crossing the Rubicon is contained in the concept of Caesar? We know it must be, for we know from history that Caesar did indeed cross the Rubicon. But to work out that containment *a priori* we need to work out why Caesar's crossing the Rubicon is part of the best possible world. But how do we do that? How do we begin to work out whether one possible world is better than another? One thing is clear, however, and that is that the analysis involved would involve multiple infinites. As Leibniz says, there is 'an infinity of possible sequences of the universe, each of which contains an infinity of creatures' (T 267).

> [E]ven if some one could know the whole series of the universe, even then he could not give a reason for it, unless he compared it with all other possibles. From this it is evident why no demonstration of a contingent proposition can be found, however far the resolution of notions is continued. (PM 99)

Despite the fact that the demonstration of contingent truths continues to infinity and is never completed Leibniz says that 'the certitude and perfect reason of contingent truths is known only to God, who grasps the infinite with one intuition' (PM 75). This has led some of Leibniz's readers to suppose that he means that there is no real objective distinction between necessity and contingency, and that the distinction is simply an appearance relative to the limited human mind. But, whether or not one finds the distinction Leibniz makes on the basis of infinite analysis satisfactory, it is not epistemological in nature. God cannot, just as we cannot, come to the end of the infinite analysis of a contingent truth. He is not able to see 'the end of the analysis ... since there is no end'. What he sees is 'the nexus of the terms or the inclusion of the predicate in the subject, since he sees everything which is in the series' (L 265).

ii. DIVINE FREEDOM

So far, in discussing human freedom, we have been supposing that God was free in his creation and that it is a contingent fact that he created the world he did create. But is this so?

Earlier we saw that one way in which it has been suggested that Leibniz tried to obtain the contingency of propositions about created substances, such as Elizabeth I's being a spinster, was to appeal to the contingency of Elizabeth's existence. The contingency of

God's creating this world, however, could not be established on the basis of contingency in God's existence. As we saw in the previous chapter, that God exists is, for Leibniz, a necessary truth.

Leibniz's 'fairy tale' obviously takes divine freedom for granted. This world, we are told, was one of an infinity of possible worlds. Being omnipotent, God could have created any of these, but in his goodness he desired to create the best, and in his wisdom he saw which this was. This account of things satisfies the three criteria which for Leibniz are constitutive of freedom: spontaneity, intelligence and contingency. First, the creation was a spontaneous and externally uncompelled act, an act of God's will. Leibniz was not alone in holding that, whatever the case with other things, God cannot be acted on by anything external to him, and that all his actions originate in himself. Secondly, the act of creation clearly involved intelligence and understanding. God evaluated the various possible worlds and judged which of them was the best. Finally, there was contingency and choice too in the creation: there was more than one world for God to decide between.

Perhaps, however, things are not as straightforward as this. There are ways in which the contingency of the actual world might seem to be threatened by the fact of its being the best. To begin, it may be said, it is not possible that a good God would do other than choose the best. Must it not be necessarily true that God chooses to actualize the best possible world?

Leibniz certainly holds that it is true that God chooses the best world. God is 'absolutely perfect', and from this it follows that he has unbounded power and knowledge and 'acts in the most perfect manner' (DM 1). But he seems to be undecided and to vacillate about whether it is necessarily or contingently true (Adams 1994: 24, 36–42). At one point he quite evidently must be thinking that it is contingent. For he says it was a free decision on God's part 'to do what is most perfect' (DM 13); and since freedom involves contingency it must be contingent that he acts in the most perfect manner and chooses the best. But elsewhere he is at any rate *inclined* to think that it is necessary that God chooses that which is the best; and it has been argued that Leibniz should be so inclined since various other features of his philosophy commit him to it (Adams 1994: 36).

In fact Leibniz was not particularly concerned that the necessity of God's choosing the best might threaten the contingency of the actual world. For he held that, whether or not it is necessarily true that God chooses the best, it is not in any case necessarily true that the actual world is the best possible. Even if we 'concede that it is necessary for God to choose the best' it does not follow, he says, 'that what is chosen is necessary' (AG 30).

Why does this not follow? Why is it not necessarily, but merely contingently true that what in fact is the best possible world is the best possible? His explanation depends on the account of contingency in terms of infinite analysis which we considered in connection with human freedom. It is, he says, only contingently true that what is the best possible world is the best because 'there is no demonstration that it is the best' (AG 30).

There is a second way in which Leibniz argued that even supposing that it is necessarily true that God wills the best, it does not follow that the actual world, with its best possible scheme of things, exists of necessity. He repeated this argument through his career, and, according to the valuation of one recent scholar, it must be regarded as Leibniz's 'principal (and most confident) solution to the problem of contingency' (Adams 1994: 12).

In effect Leibniz faces the objection that this actual world, which is the best possible, is really the *only* possible world. Given that 'God wills the best through his nature' and so 'wills by necessity', 'surely it follows from this that things exist by necessity' (AG 20). His response is that it does not follow, for the other possible, but less good worlds, 'remain possible, even if God did not choose them'. Certainly such a less good world is 'not possible with respect to the divine will'; but it 'remains possible in its nature'. It 'implies no contradiction, even though its coexistence with God can in some way be said to imply a contradiction' (AG 21). For this world to be contingent it is sufficient that, even if it were not possible for God to choose them, there are other worlds possible in themselves, worlds which involve no contradiction. With respect to God's omnipotent power their creation was certainly possible.

But if these other worlds, possible though they may be in themselves and with respect to God's power, are 'not possible in respect of the divine will' is it really proper to speak of God's making a choice? Leibniz thinks that it is. There is, he said 'no necessity in the object of God's choice'. What he chose, though of course possible *in itself*, was not necessary *of itself*. There were a number of other worlds, possible in themselves, between which to choose. God's choice was not forced in that there were no alternatives. This means that the choice was 'free and independent of necessity' (T 148).

The question must inevitably arise as to whether Leibniz succeeds in his various attempts to defend contingency and justify the claim that God's creation of the world was a free act. An important element in all that he says is, it has been argued, a keen desire to establish a distance between himself and the necessitarianism which he saw in Spinoza. In judging his attempts to defend contingency we should therefore see him in this light and allow him 'to disagree with Spinoza in his own way rather than in some way that we might impose on him' (Adams 1994: 20–1).

On Leibniz's reading of him, Spinoza believed in 'a metaphysical necessity in events' (T 236), and held that 'the world could not have been produced by God in any other way than it has been produced' (L 204); in short, Spinoza believed that this world was the only logically or metaphysically possible world. So Leibniz's claim that 'there is no necessity in the object of God's choice', in that there are many different worlds possible in themselves, is one clear way in which he differs from Spinoza. It is, of course, an essential part of his claim that God has some conception and understanding of various degrees of goodness of these alternatives from which he makes his choice. It is, that is to say, essential to Leibniz's account that God has an intellect. For Spinoza, however, not merely are there no alternatives between which to choose, for this world is the only world possible in itself, but also his God is not possessed of intellect and understanding in any usual sense. According to Spinoza there is nothing in common but the name between intellect as usually understood and God's 'intellect'. There is, he held, about as much similarity between them as there is between a dog, the animal that barks, and the celestial constellation called the Dog. Spinoza's God differs from Leibniz's in respect also of lacking will in any ordinary sense; and it is because his God is impersonal in these ways that his necessitarianism is what Leibniz describes as 'geometrical' (T 348) 'blind' (T 234) or 'brute' (T 348). Spinoza seems, he said, to have 'taught a blind necessity, having denied to the Author of Things understanding and will, and assumed that good and perfection relate to us only and not to him' (T 234). Spinoza destroyed 'freedom and contingency', for he thought that what happens is the only thing possible, and 'must happen by a brute geometrical necessity'. Spinoza also 'divested God of intelligence and choice, leaving him a blind power, whence all emanates of necessity' (T 348).

Leibniz's account of God's creation of the world is free of the necessitarianism which he wants to avoid, because involved in it are understanding, will and rational choice between alternatives which differ in their degree of objective goodness. In his creation, Leibniz's God acts freely, for he is faced with a choice and that choice is made through his will and desire for goodness:

> it is true freedom, and the most perfect, to be able to make the best use of one's free will ... Although [God's] will is always indefectible and always tends towards the best, the evil or the lesser good which he rejects will still be possible in itself. Otherwise the necessity of good would be geometrical (so to speak) or metaphysical, and altogether absolute; the contingency of things would be destroyed, and there would be no choice. (T 386–7)

FURTHER READING

There is a very large body of literature on the topics discussed in this chapter; from it the following may be mentioned:

On freedom generally, both human and divine: Borst (1992), Frankel (1984), Greenberg (2005), Johnson (1954), Nason (1942: 22–8), Parkinson (1970), Phemister (1991); on God's freedom specifically, Adams (1994: 36–42), Blumenfeld (1975), Gale (1976), Resnik (1973); on human spontaneity: Murray (2005), Rutherford (2005).

For Leibniz's different accounts of contingency see Abraham (1969), Adams (1994: ch. 1), Curley (1972), Ishiguro (1979a), Jarrett (1978), Meijering (1978), Russell (1900: chs. 2, 3). On the idea of 'contingent containment' specifically, see Adams (1994: 30–4), Sleigh (1990a: 64–7), Vailati (1986: 330–39). For the infinite analysis account of contingency see Adams (1994: 25–30), Blumenfeld (1984–1985), Carriero (1993, 1995), Sleigh (1990a: ch. 4, sect. 8). For the idea of things being 'possible in themselves' see Adams (1994: 12–20), Blumenfeld (1988), Resnik (1973), Sleigh (1990a: ch. 4, sect. 7).

CHAPTER 12

THE BEST OF ALL POSSIBLE WORLDS

The preceding chapters have reviewed various details and aspects of what Russell called Leibniz's 'philosophical edifice'; they have looked at the underlying ideas of his culminating 'fantastic fairy tale'. If only one thing were known about that 'edifice' it would probably be its doctrine that God created the best world that it was possible to create. This world is the best possible world, Leibniz held, 'which God knows through his wisdom, chooses through his goodness, and produces through his power' (Mon 55).

In what way is it the best? Leibniz is quite positive that goodness and beauty are not dependent on human judgement. He rejects the idea, which he attributes to Spinoza, that 'the beauty of the universe and the goodness that we attribute to the works of God are no more than the chimeras of men' (DM 2). He is in agreement with Descartes about this, according to whom the 'the nature of all goodness ... is already determined' (CSM 2.292) *from the human point of view*. According to Descartes, however, from the *Divine* point of view it is not already determined. For him the nature of goodness is determined *by God*. Just as (we saw in Chapter 10) essential or necessary truths are, in Descartes' view, fixed according as God wills, so too is goodness: things count as good because God decided they do. 'The reason for their goodness depends on the fact that he exercised his will to make them so' (CSM 2.294). Leibniz, however, found it 'altogether strange' to hold that 'the rules of goodness, justice and perfection are no more than the effects of God's will' (DM 2). They are, he insists, independent of and prior to God's will; what counts as the best is not a matter of God's choice, any more than it is a matter of ours. So what makes this world the best is not simply that it is the one God chose. God chose it because he judged by his understanding that it was. Its being the best and the reasons for its goodness were prior to God's picking it out as the best.

In what way, then, is this *the best* out of all possible worlds? We might wonder at the outset why it is *the* best. Why might not there be two equally best possible worlds? Leibniz's principle of sufficient reason provides a reason why not. If there were, then God would have had no reason for choosing between them, would not have chosen between them, and so would have created nothing.

We are not able of course to see in detail just why this world is the best; that it is the best is, as we saw in the last chapter, a contingent truth the demonstration of which requires an infinite analysis. It is beyond our finite minds to have detailed knowledge of the particular reasons which led God to choose the universe he did. But, Leibniz thinks, we are able say something in general concerning the objective criteria of goodness, justice and perfection, on the basis of which God judged and chose this world.

i. THE BEST WORLD METAPHYSICALLY OR NATURALLY

In fact there are different sets of criteria for, Leibniz says, our world is the best 'not only in the metaphysical sense', but also 'morally speaking' (DM 1). Associated with God's creation being both 'metaphysically' and 'morally' the best are two distinct ways in which God is related to it: there is, as we saw in Chapter 10, a Kingdom of Nature and a Kingdom of Ends. God is related to the world as an expert architect or designer, and also as a monarch and moral legislator.

Regarding the 'metaphysical perfection' of the world seen as a Kingdom of Nature, Leibniz says that in producing the best possible world God balanced simplicity of means against the variety, richness and abundance of effects produced by those means. God, he said, was like an architect who balances the money available for a building against its desired size and beauty: he wants the most in respect of the end with the least in respect of the means. So in choosing the most perfect world God chose 'the one that is simultaneously the simplest in hypotheses and richest in phenomena' (DM 6). Both of these things, simplicity and richness, are of value in their own right, so that if greater richness could be produced by less simple means, by more complex hypotheses, this would not necessarily be better: 'the *means* are also in a sense *ends* ... they are desirable not only on account of what they do, but on account of what they are' (T 257). Taking up the metaphor of the architect, Leibniz says that 'more intricate processes take up too much ground, too much space, too much place, too much time that might have been better employed' (T 257). God, then, has so structured the Kingdom of Nature, the natural world as studied by the physical sciences, in such a way that a 'variety, richness or abundance' (DM 5) of natural effects and phenomena has been produced by the simplest of laws of nature.

Leibniz does not say a lot about what exactly he means by 'simplicity'. In a rare comment he says that 'the simpler system is always preferred in astronomy' (DM 5), and presumably he has in mind here that the hypothesis of the sixteenth-century astronomer Copernicus that the earth travels round the sun is preferable to the complexities required to maintain the earlier Ptolemaic system according to which the earth is at the centre of things. Besides characterizing them as simple, however, Leibniz says other, perhaps not unconnected things, about the physical laws by which God governs the Kingdom of Nature.

He speaks of them being 'universal' and free from exceptions. In his wisdom God always acts *according to principles*; always *according to rules*, and never *according to exceptions*' (T 328). Thus, it has been suggested as an example, Newton's law of gravitation would count for Leibniz as having quite a high degree of universality in that it applies to not only planetary motions, but also to phenomena which at first sight seem quite different: the tidal movement of the sea, and the falling of bodies (Rutherford 1995a: 27). In regulating a wide range of apparently disparate phenomena the law could be seen as productive of a richer world.

Perhaps intending to give more content to the idea of 'simplicity', Leibniz says that God's laws of nature are efficient and such that the 'greatest effect should be produced with ... the least expenditure' (PM 138). The phenomena of nature are always produced 'by the simplest and most determinate ways' (DM 21). An example is the fact that water drops tend to take up a spherical shape – the shape which gives them the smallest surface area for their volume. Another example illustrates Leibniz's explanatory expansion of this principle. In going from one point to another then, unless there is something more 'to determine the way', we will chose the path 'that is easiest or shortest' (PM 138). Leibniz found an understanding of that principle at work in the discovery earlier in his century of the laws of reflection and refraction of light by the physicists Snell and Fermat. In making their discoveries they assumed that nature was so designed that light would travel through a medium by the easiest or most determinate route. Descartes' demonstration of what has become known as Snell's law did not involve any such insight and consequently, said Leibniz, it was nothing like as good.

God's 'supreme wisdom' in creating the metaphysically best possible world in which 'the greatest effect is produced by the simplest means' is further illustrated by reference to the conservation laws of motion which were discussed in Chapter 6. Without much explanation he says that God has chosen them because they are 'best adjusted and the most fitted to abstract and metaphysical reasons' (PNG 11). The idea is also illustrated by what Leibniz calls 'the law of continuity' according to which changes in nature never take place 'by a leap' (La 668–9). He says that this 'principle of general order ... is effective in physics ... because the sovereign wisdom, the source of all things, acts ... observing a harmony' (L 351).

Leibniz saw the principle as 'a test or criterion' by which suggested laws of nature could be examined. He demonstrated that the detailed laws which Descartes proposed for collisions between moving bodies violate it. He showed that they involve irregularities and gaps, which a good and wise God would never have chosen to produce. (For illustrations of these leaps and discontinuities in Descartes' collision rules see Woolhouse and Francks 1998: 177–9.)

Besides being the most simple in respect of laws, the best possible world excels in the variety and abundance of its phenomena. Extolling the value of variety Leibniz comments that King Midas turned out to be less rich when he had only gold. It is superfluous to multiply the same thing. The principle of the identity of indiscernibles is a guarantee of variety. The way to obtain as much variety as possible is for there to be an 'infinite multitude of simple substances' (Mon 57); for since each of these has its own perspective or point of view on the world, 'it is as if there were so many different universes' (Mon 57). But the 'variety' Leibniz has in mind is perhaps not just one of a multitude of individual substances but also one of greatest possible number of species. It is suitable to 'the magnificent harmony' of the universe, and in accordance with the law of continuity, that there is a series of closely resembling species, ranging in degrees of perfection from the lowest creatures, through human beings, upwards towards God (NE 306–7).

The Kingdom of Nature of this, the best possible world, is, then, not only the 'simplest in hypotheses' but also the 'richest in phenomena' (DM 6). How do these two different criteria compare or play off against each other? It has been suggested that there is a conflict between them. A less varied world (one whose only animal life was the amoeba, say) would require a simpler structure of laws than one with a more complex fauna. Perhaps, then, simplicity and richness vary inversely. If so, then any world must involve a trade-off between them, and the physically best possible world will be the one in which the sum of the two is at a maximum. In this case the best possible world may well not be the richest possible in phenomena, nor the simplest possible in hypotheses, *when those characteristics are taken in isolation*. What it will be, however, is the world where the sum of these two is at a maximum and greater than in any other possible world.

A further and different suggestion has been made about the relation of the two criteria. When Leibniz says that God chose the world which is the simplest in its laws and the richest in its phenomena he does not have in mind that these values 'pull in opposite directions'. He does not have in mind that simplicity and richness are adjusted to each other, and in the best possible world are at the maximum possible in relation to each other. Rather, he means just what he says: that the best possible world is *the simplest* possible world, *and* is *the richest* possible world. This interpretation has to ignore Leibniz's saying that the two criteria are to be 'balanced against' (DM 5) each other, as when an architect balances his budget against the brief for his building. But in its favour are texts according to which simplicity, so far from 'pulling against' richness, is actually productive of it. Richness and variety, Leibniz says in places, is achieved precisely by the use of simple laws. 'God makes the maximum of things he can, and what obliges him to seek simple laws is precisely the necessity to find place for as many things as can be put together' (L 211).

Besides explaining metaphysical perfection in terms of simplicity of laws and richness and variety of phenomena, Leibniz explains it in other terms too. A metaphysically perfect world is one which is completely harmonious. In such a world 'everything is regulated in things once for all with as much order and agreement as possible' (PNG 13). Such a world is also one that contains 'the greatest amount of essence or positive reality'. Metaphysically or physically this world is the best possible, he says, in that 'that series of things will be forthcoming which in actual fact affords the greatest quantity of reality' (PM 141). Finally, it is the world which has the greatest 'degree of affirmative intelligibility' (AG 230); it contains a maximum of things worthy of investigation and offering scope for the exercise of our reason and scientific endeavours.

However, as Leibniz scholars have made clear, these further and perhaps seemingly disparate characterizations of the best possible world are not unrelated to those of simplicity and richness. For example, and briefly, a world which is richer and more varied in that it contains a larger number of individuals is also one which contains a greater amount of essence. A world which has a high degree of what Leibniz calls 'affirmative intelligibility' is one which is subject to simpler laws which cover a larger number of phenomena. It is a matter of some debate, however, whether these further criteria are, or are not, more basic than those of simplicity and richness.

ii. THE BEST WORLD MORALLY

Besides being metaphysically or naturally the best possible, this world is *morally* the best too. This means that there is conferred on minds or rational spirits 'the greatest possible amount of felicity and joyfulness' (PM 141). There is, however, some continuity between the two kinds of perfection, that of the Kingdom of Nature, and that of the Kingdom of Ends, or of Grace. Though happiness is only possible for self-aware beings, beings capable of reflection, it 'is to persons what perfection is to beings [in general]'. The 'first principle' behind the existence of the physical world is that it has 'the greatest possible perfection', while that of 'the moral world or City of God ... must be to spread as much happiness as possible in it' (DM 36).

On occasion Leibniz says that 'the whole universe is made only to contribute to ... the happiness' of rational beings (LA 125). We concern God 'infinitely more' than all other beings (DM 35). Other things simply serve as our tools, or instruments for our happiness. The reason why God has 'the most care of minds' (DM 36) is that of all the things he created we are most like God, for he is a mind. We are 'made in His image', we are as 'children of His house' (DM 36). Our possession of rationality brings us close to the divinity in various ways. As we saw in Chapter 5, rational minds are the only beings with free will, and so the only ones that can serve God freely. Moreover, in having understanding, we can have knowledge of necessary truths and acquire an understanding of the universe. All substances (as we saw in Chapter 3) express the whole world, but we also know and understand the world, and so we express God as well as the world. Finally, the fact that we are as near to the divinity as it is possible for created things to be means that God gets more glory from us than from any other part of his creation. It is because of this that he, as a prince, enters into society with us, as subjects.

At other times, however (and certainly towards the end of his life) Leibniz is less enthusiastically anthropomorphic than this. Though he is quite clear that the happiness of rational beings is *one* of God's main aims, he steps down from saying it is his sole aim. If we find things in the universe which are not pleasing to us we should remember that it is not made for us alone. God certainly values a man more than a lion, Leibniz said, but it is not so certain that he 'prefers a single man in all respects to the whole of lion-kind' (T 188). Even if he did he would not go so far as to prefer the interest of a number of people over 'general disorder diffused through an infinite number of creatures' (T 189).

In fact even in the places where Leibniz stresses the importance of the moral perfection of the happiness of minds, it is plain that the world's being morally the best does not take precedence over its being metaphysically the best. It is not that minds have the greatest possible happiness taken by itself and in isolation. It is rather that they have the greatest that 'the universal harmony can permit' (DM 36). The aim that the moral world, the city of God, should contain the greatest possible happiness does not trump the aim that the physical world should have the greatest possible perfection.

Some people have read Leibniz as holding not merely that moral perfection does not trump metaphysical or physical perfection but, even more strongly, that metaphysical perfection is the more important of the two (Russell 1900: 199, Couturat (see Parkinson 1965: 114–15)). In fact, though, the situation with respect to the two kinds of perfection parallels the one we saw earlier with respect to the two criteria of metaphysical perfection, simplicity of laws and richness of phenomena. We saw then that Leibniz's view is that simplicity, so far from pulling against richness, is actually productive of it. We must see now that his view is that metaphysical perfection is a means to human happiness. There is, that is to say, a harmony between metaphysical and moral perfection.

Happiness, on Leibniz's understanding of it, is a state of permanent pleasure. Of course, a happy person does not feel this pleasure at every instant: being in a state of permanent pleasure does not involve being continuously pleased, any more than believing something involves continuously acting on or expressing the belief. It is, rather, that a happy person is one who is disposed to feel pleasure. What then is pleasure, that thing whose permanence is happiness?

When we derive pleasure from something which appeals to us, whether it be a piece of music or some tasty food, we are, in Leibniz's view, responding to some harmony, fitness and order in it. Pleasure, he maintains, is 'the feeling of a perfection or an excellence' (L 425). When we experience pleasant sensations, as from music or food, we don't know rationally just what the perfection or excellence which pleases us consists in. We are simply responding to it without knowing why.

The way to happiness as a state of permanent pleasure is of course through pleasure. But sensory pleasures and appetites are not necessarily the way to it. They are temporary and fleeting and by themselves they may lead only to further temporary pleasures and not to the permanent state which is happiness. They may even not do that. In 'rushing straight at a present pleasure', for example some appetizing food, we sometimes can, Leibniz points out, 'fall into the abyss of misery' (NE 189). Food which tastes good may be unhealthy. Leibniz advocates, then, that sensory enjoyment must be governed by reason and understanding, in the way that the exercise we take or our diet should be.

In fact it is precisely reason and understanding, and the pleasures associated with them, that take us from temporary pleasure to happiness. Sometimes we do understand how the perfection and order, which pleases us and to which we respond, is constituted and produced. We may, for example, have some understanding of musical theory, of composition and harmony, some understanding of how sounds are to be combined in a pleasing way; and such understanding of why a certain piece of music is pleasing *is itself pleasing*, Leibniz holds. Moreover, pleasures of this further kind, pleasures which involve the understanding and are not purely sensory, pleasures which stem from 'the knowledge ... of order and harmony, are the most valuable' (NE 194). They are steps on the road, not to further temporary pleasures, but to the permanent state of pleasure which is happiness. '[N]othing serves our happiness better than the illumination of our understanding and the exercise of our will to act always according to our understanding' (L 426).

In what way, then, is there a harmony between metaphysical perfection and moral perfection? How is metaphysical perfection a means to the moral goodness of happiness as Leibniz conceives it? A metaphysically perfect world is, we have seen, one of richness and variety produced by simple laws which cover a large number of phenomena. As such it is a world which has a high degree of what Leibniz calls 'affirmative intelligibility'. It follows that a metaphysically perfect world is such as to afford great scope for the rational pleasures and happiness which can be got from a knowledge and understanding of its order and harmony. '[T]he world is a cosmos, full of ornament; that is ... made in such a way that it gives the greatest satisfaction to an intelligent being' (PM 146). Experiencing rational pleasures and gaining happiness from increasing our knowledge and understanding of the perfections of the kingdom of nature involves the exercise of our intellectual abilities. In this exercise we are increasing in our own perfection, and perception of this too (both in ourselves and others) is something from which we derive further pleasure and happiness (Rutherford 1995a: 51).

As explained above, God values spirits or minds because, of all his creation, they are most like him. Like him, but to a lesser degree, they have rationality and understanding; and, as such, they are able to come to a knowledge and appreciation of the world he has created. A metaphysically perfect world, we have just seen, offers great scope for the exercise of this ability (and for the rational pleasures derived from that exercise). This is at least part of what Leibniz has in mind when, in explaining the importance of rational spirits to God, he says that other things are made for them.

The perfection of minds 'consists in felicity and joyfulness' (PM 141), but there are two aspects to this. One is the ability to come to an appreciation and understanding of the metaphysical perfection of the kingdom of nature, to 'knowledge of truth'. The other is the 'exercise of virtue' (L 219). This too is a source of the good of happiness. Like the knowledge of truth, moral goodness or virtue requires the use of reason, for it is 'a disposition to act in accordance with reason' (NE 98), but it is more important than knowledge and is 'the noblest quality of created things' (T 198).

In creating the best possible world God has seen to it that virtue is rewarded by happiness and sins are punished.

[T]he very law of justice itself ... dictates that each should have a part in the perfection of the universe and in his own happiness in proportion to his own virtue and the extent to which his will is directed towards the common good. (PM 143)

When Leibniz assures us that crimes never go unpunished or good actions without suitable reward he recognizes that this 'cannot and ought not always to happen immediately' (Mon 89). He has in mind, of course, the happiness and suffering in 'the great future' (PNG 16, 18), some time after our physical death. Yet besides the future happiness and reward for virtue which the Bible's revelations promise there is also immediate happiness to be gained from the practice of virtue and the direction of our will towards the common good. We take pleasure in the happiness of others, and in doing what seems to conform to God's will. Thus we bring upon ourselves 'new joys by new progress in goodness' (T 162). Finally, there is pleasure and happiness to be got from love of God:

God is the most perfect ... and consequently the most loveable of substances, and since *pure true love* consists in the state which causes pleasure to be felt in the perfections ... of the beloved, this love ought to give us the greatest pleasure of which a man is capable. (PNG 16)

iii. EVIL IN THE BEST POSSIBLE WORLD

In 1755, nearly forty years after Leibniz's death, a huge earthquake (since estimated at magnitude 9) struck and largely destroyed Lisbon, the capital of Portugal, killing somewhere between 10,000 and a 100,000 of its inhabitants. Voltaire, the French *philosophe*, horrified, was struck by the apparent incompatibility between this event and the optimism of Leibniz's claim that God created the best of all possible worlds. He lampooned it in his novel *Candide* (Voltaire 1758): crawling among the ruins, Candide, 'terrified ... weltering in blood and trembling with fear and confusion ... said to himself "If this is the best of all possible worlds, what can the rest be like?" ' (Voltaire 1758: ch. 6).

Of course it took neither Leibniz's 'bold and paradoxical opinion' (as Hume called it) that this is, both metaphysically and morally, the best of all possible worlds, nor the Lisbon earthquake to stimulate people to wonder what conclusion should be drawn from the obvious evil and undeserved suffering in the world (Hume 1779: X). People had long asked how, given such sufferings, there can be a divine creator. If there is an omniscient God it seems that either he is not omnipotent or he is not good. The ancient Greek philosopher Epicurus put the dilemma well: God 'either wishes to take away evils and he cannot, or he can and does not wish to'. In the first case he is not omnipotent, 'which does not fall in with the notion of God'; in the second case he is malicious, 'which is equally foreign to God'. But if 'he both wishes to and is able, which alone is fitting to God, whence, therefore, are there evils, and why does he not remove them?' (reported by Lactantius 313: ch. 13). Leibniz acknowledged the force of this last question and towards the end of his life wrote and published a lengthy work, *Theodicy*, devoted to answering it.

Different things need to be said about different evils, for of these there are, Leibniz says, three different sorts: metaphysical, physical, and moral. '*Metaphysical evil* consists in mere imperfection, *physical evil* in suffering, and *moral evil* in sin' (T 136). Despite the fact that he sometimes calls it 'natural', Leibniz's 'physical evil' is not the same as what is usually called 'natural evil'. The Lisbon earthquake (as opposed to, say, the holocaust of the second World War) would be an example of what is often called a 'natural evil', but is not what Leibniz would have called a 'physical' evil; for him what would have been physical evil would have been the pain and suffering which the earthquake caused. The holocaust, however, would for Leibniz as for us have counted as a moral evil, a sinful event brought about, unlike the earthquake, by humans. It was, of course, similar to the earthquake in that it also resulted in the physical evil of pain and suffering.

Though for Leibniz this world is metaphysically the best possible, he does not claim that it is metaphysically perfect and without metaphysical evil. For one thing, the created beings which compose it are not metaphysically perfect. If they were they would all be alike, and this would mean that the world lacked richness and variety, something which is 'neither fitting nor possible' (T 135). For another thing, simply by virtue of being created the things in the world are limited and imperfect. 'There is', Leibniz said, 'an *original imperfection in the creature*' because a created thing 'is limited in its essence' (T 135). A metaphysically perfect thing would be divine, and if created things were Gods 'it would not have been possible to produce them' (T 252), they would have existed necessarily.

So, even the best possible world is going to be metaphysically imperfect. This inevitable element of metaphysical evil in the created world is indeed the source of the other evils in it. It is because created beings are limited and imperfect that there is the moral evil of sin. There is 'a limitation or original imperfection common to the natures of all creatures making them capable of sin or liable to fail' (DM 30). This original imperfection is not the 'original sin' which stems from Adam's sin; it is something to which Adam himself, as a created being, was subject before his fall, and something which itself was instrumental in his fall. It is indeed an imperfection which we, as rational spirits, share with all lower creatures. But, properly speaking, this does not mean that *all* creatures are liable to *sin*. As we saw in Chapter 11, only rational spirits have freewill, and as such only they are capable of and have the freedom to sin, only they are susceptible to praise and blame.

In its turn, the moral evil of sin, says Leibniz, is a source of natural evil. Clearly this is so, whether we think of the pain and suffering which people sometimes directly and intentionally inflict, or of that which can result indirectly from actions such as theft or unthinking neglect. Indeed what is evil about moral evil is, he says, precisely that it does produce natural evil. '[M]oral evil is an evil so great only because it is a source of physical evils' (T 138). Nevertheless, the undeserved sufferings we have through the sins of others 'prepare for us', Leibniz says (presumably thinking of the afterlife), 'a greater happiness' (T 276). Moral evil is only one source of natural evil, though. For, as noted above, the natural evil of pain and suffering often has its source in natural phenomena such as earthquakes and floods.

Though any created world, even the best possible, must contain metaphysical evil, and though moral and natural evils result from this original imperfection, they are not absolutely inevitable consequences of it. Though this, the best possible world, contains such evils they are not, according to Leibniz, a part of any possible world. There are, that is to say, possible worlds which are free from moral and natural evil. It would have been convenient for Leibniz if he had thought otherwise, for he would then have had a ready explanation of the presence of such evil in our world, the best possible world. He could have explained them by saying that they are a part of this world because they must be a part of any possible world. What he does say, however, is that though such evils are not inevitable as such, they are, perhaps rather surprisingly, *an inevitable part of the best possible world*. We can, Leibniz allows, imagine possible worlds without sin and unhappiness; but they would, he assures us, be 'be very inferior to ours in goodness' (T 129).

Quite clearly there is a pressing problem for Leibniz here. If worlds are possible in which evil is avoided then why does it form part of the best possible world? It is certainly not Leibniz's view that we should be pleased by or welcome, the occurrence of sin and suffering; though it is, nevertheless, sometimes the case that an evil produces a good. We should remember, for example, that 'we have gained Jesus Christ himself by reason of sin' (T 130).

One kind of world in which there would be no moral evil, no sin, would be a world in which there was nothing capable of sin. This would be a world in which there were no spirits, no rational minds, no beings with free will, no Kingdom of God in fact. Leibniz allows that such a world is possible, but, as we have seen, a world without minds would not be the best possible. Minds, we saw, 'are the most perfectible of all substances', so God 'who always looks to the greatest perfection in general, will have the most care of minds' (DM 36).

Before creation, God's will was to create the best possible world; his intention was to create the world which his understanding showed him to be the best. But though God 'loves virtue supremely and hates vice supremely' some moral evils, Leibniz explains, *had to be permitted* (T 266). They were not evils which he directly willed, rather they were ones which were 'involved in the best plan for the universe' (T 260). God has a very strong reason for permitting and tolerating evils: 'Not only does he derive from them greater goods, but he finds them connected with the greatest goods of all those that are possible' (T 200). It would, therefore, be a fault if he did not permit them. This however applies only to moral evils. With the natural evils of pain and suffering the case is different. Sometimes God does will them directly (not just permit them), as a punishment, or as a means to preventing greater evils or to obtaining a greater good. Summing all of this up Leibniz says that, directly and as an end, God wills only the good. Moral evil is never willed directly. Sometimes God directly wills natural evil, either as a punishment, or as a means to some better end. Moral evil, however, is only ever permitted indirectly or permissively, as being connected in some way with the best (T 137–8).

Evils, both natural and moral, are inevitable, then, in the best possible world. But while we have to accept that we cannot hope to understand the order of the world well enough to see that it was indeed 'impossible to make it better than it is' (Mon 90), Leibniz tries in various ways to make it easier to accept the presence of these evils. As just noted, natural evils can sometimes be justified as a means to an end, and though moral evils can never be justified in this way, they are sometimes mitigated by their effects, such as Christ's coming. So far as human life is concerned he is 'bold to say that we shall find, upon unbiased scrutiny of the facts, that taking all in all human life is in general tolerable' (T 286).

Leibniz urges optimism too about the universe in general and as a whole. He is confident that in the universe not only does 'the good exceed the evil, but also the evil serves to augment the good' (T 263). He points out that we are not well placed to see this. We know only a very limited part of the universe, and know it during a very limited part of its total history. What we know of it is almost as nothing compared with what is unknown to us. It could well be that all the evils we know are 'almost nothingness in comparison with the good things which are in the universe' (T 135).

In pointing out that our knowledge of the universe is limited Leibniz sometimes has in mind not just that we are in no position to see that the good exceeds the evil. His thought is also that we cannot see how the evil we know of may in fact 'augment' (T 263) and contribute to the good of the whole, taken not just as the sum of its parts, but as a harmonious whole. 'The part of the best Whole is not of necessity the best that one could have made of this part. For the part of a beautiful thing is not always beautiful' (T 261). Some of the analogies he uses to illustrate this idea imply that a less than perfect element of a more perfect whole really is less than perfect in itself. He points out, for example, that sweet things may need to be accompanied by bitter things if the sweetness is not to be insipid. He points out, too, that imperfections may be necessary for us to appreciate good. 'He who has not tasted what is bitter has not earned what is sweet, nor will he appreciate it' (PM 143). 'We may take pleasure in ... the experience of ills, from the very sense or proof they give us of our own power or felicity' (PM 142).

At other times, however, his analogies suggest a different way in which evil may 'serve to augment the good'. They suggest that we should think of an evil or imperfection not as an imperfect but necessary part of a perfect whole but rather as something which, from a limited standpoint, merely *appears* as an imperfection. A small part of a picture looked at closely may look like 'aimless smear', a 'confused medley of colours, without selection, without art'. But, when looked at as a whole and from the right distance the picture will be seen to have been 'accomplished with the highest art' (PM 142). Similarly, he refers to 'devices of perspective' in which certain 'designs look like mere confusion until one restores them to the right angle of vision'. He has in mind here so-called anamorphic art of which Hans Holbein's painting 'The Ambassadors' provides an example. In this, the shapeless mass towards the bottom of the picture turns out, when viewed at a slant, to be a grinning skull. Thus, Leibniz says, the *'apparent* deformities of our little worlds combine to become beauties in the great world' (T 216, italics added).

FURTHER READING

Metaphysical or Natural Perfection

Criteria of simplicity and richness: Blumenfeld (1995b: 382–93), Brown (1988), Gale (1976), Rescher (1969, 1981: ch. 1), Rutherford (1995a: ch. 2). Further criteria: Blumenfeld (1995b: 393–8), Gale (1976), Rutherford (1995a: ch. 2).

Moral Perfection

Pleasure, happiness, virtue: Blumenfeld (1995b: 398–405), Brown (1988), Hostler (1975: chs. 5–7), Rutherford (1995a: ch. 3).
Evil and the best possible world: Hostler (1975: chs. 8–9), Wilson (1983).

ABBREVIATIONS AND REFERENCES

i. ABBREVIATIONS USED IN REFERENCES

AG: Ariew and Garber 1989.
CSM: Cottingham *et al.* 1970 (cited by volume and page).
DM: Leibniz 1686.
K: Kenny 1970.
L: Loemker 1969.
La: Langley 1949.
LA: Leibniz 1686–1690.
LC: Leibniz 1715–1716.
Mon: Leibniz 1714b.
NE: Leibniz 1703–1705.
NI: Leibniz 1698.
NS: Leibniz 1695.
PM: Parkinson and Morris 1973.
PNG: Leibniz 1714a.
T: Leibniz 1710.
WF: Woolhouse and Francks 1997.

ii. REFERENCES

Abraham, William E. (1969), 'Complete concepts and Leibniz's distinction between necessary and contingent propositions', *Studia Leibnitiana*, 1, 263–79.

Adams, Robert Merrihew (1994), *Leibniz: Determinist, Theist, Idealist*. New York: Oxford University Press.

Aiton, E. J. (1985), *Leibniz: A Biography*. Bristol: Adam Hilger.

Alexander, H. G. (1956), *The Leibniz-Clarke Correspondence*. Manchester: Manchester University Press.

Alexander, Peter (1985), *Ideas, Qualities, and Corpuscles: Locke and Boyle on the External World*. Cambridge: Cambridge University Press.

Alles, Adam (1933), 'Leibniz's dual conception of human reason', reprinted in Woolhouse 1994, vol. 4, pp. 60–6, from *The Personalist*, 14, 177–84.

Antognazza, Maria Rosa (2008), *Leibniz: An Intellectual Biography*. New York: Cambridge University Press.

Aquinas, Thomas (1964), *Summa Theologiae*, in Thomas Gilby and T. C. O'Brien (eds). London: Eyre and Spottiswoode.

Ariew, Roger (1995), 'G.W. Leibniz, life and works', in Jolley 1995, pp. 18–42.

——, and Garber, Daniel (1989), *G. W. Leibniz: Philosophical Essays*. Indianapolis, IN: Hackett.

Aristotle (1941), *Categories*, in Richard McKeon (ed.), *The Works of Aristotle*. New York: Random House.

Ayer, A. J. (1936), *Language, Truth and Logic*. London: Gollancz.

Bayle, Pierre (1696), Note H to 'Rorarius', *Historical and Critical Dictionary*, in Woolhouse and Francks 1997, pp. 72–5.

—— (1702), Note L to 'Rorarius', *Historical and Critical Dictionary*, in Woolhouse and Francks 1997, pp. 86–96.

Bennett, Jonathan (2005), '*Leibniz's Two Realms*', in Rutherford and Cover 2005, pp. 135–55.

Berkeley, George (1710), *Principles of Human Knowledge*, in Roger Woolhouse (ed.) (1988), *George Berkeley: Principles of Human Knowledge/Three Dialogues*. London: Penguin.

Bernstein, Howard R. (1981), 'Passivity and inertia in Leibniz's *dynamics*', reprinted in Woolhouse 1994, vol. 3, pp. 273–88, from *Studia Leibnitiana*, 13, 97–113.

Blumenfeld, David (1972), 'Leibniz's modal proof of the possibility of God', *Studia Leibnitiana*, 4, 132–40.

—— (1973), 'Leibniz's theory of the striving possibles', reprinted in Woolhouse 1994, vol. 2, pp. 1–13, from *Studia Leibnitiana*, 5, 163–77.

—— (1975), 'Is the best possible world possible?', *Philosophical Review*, 84, 163–77.

—— (1984–1985), 'Leibniz on contingency and infinite analysis', *Philosophy and Phenomenological Research*, 45, 483–514.

—— (1988), 'Freedom, contingency, and things possible in themselves', reprinted in Woolhouse 1994, vol. 4, pp. 303–22, from *Philosophy and Phenomenological Research*, 49, 81–101.

—— (1995a), 'Leibniz's ontological and cosmological arguments', in Jolley 1995, pp. 353–81.

—— (1995b), 'Perfection and happiness in the best possible world', in Jolley 1995, pp. 382–410.

Borst, Clive (1992), 'Leibniz and the compatibilist account of free will', *Studia Leibnitiana*, 24, 49–58.

Boyle, Robert (1666), *Origin of Forms and Qualities*, in M. A. Stewart (ed.) (1979), *Selected Philosophical Papers of Robert Boyle*. Manchester: Manchester University Press.

Brandom, Robert B. (1981), 'Leibniz and degrees of perception', reprinted in Woolhouse 1994, vol. 4, pp. 117–49, from *Journal of the History of Philosophy*, 19, 447–79.

Broad, C. D. (1946), 'Leibniz's last controversy with the Newtonians', reprinted in Woolhouse 1994, vol. 3, pp. 1–19, from *Theoria*, 12, 143–68.

—— (1975), *Leibniz: An Introduction*. Cambridge: Cambridge University Press.

Brody, Baruch (1977), 'Leibniz's metaphysical logic', reprinted in Woolhouse 1994, vol. 1, pp. 82–96, from *Rice University Studies*, 63, no. 4, 43–55.

Brown, Gregory (1988), 'Leibniz's Theodicy and the confluence of worldly goods', reprinted in Woolhouse 1994, vol. 4, pp. 451–72, from *Journal of the History of Philosophy*, 26, 571–91.

Buchdahl, Gerd (1969), *Metaphysics and the Philosophy of Science*. Oxford: Basil Blackwell.

Carriero, John (1993), 'Leibniz on infinite resolution and intra-mundane contingency', *Studia Leibnitiana*, 25, 1–26.

—— (1995), 'Leibniz on infinite resolution and intra-mundane contingency', *Studia Leibnitiana*, 27, 1–30.

Chernoff, Fred (1981), 'Leibniz's principle of the identity of indiscernibles', reprinted in Woolhouse 1994, vol. 3, pp. 112–26, from *Philosophical Quarterly*, 31, 126–38.

Clagett, Marshall (1959), *The Science of Mechanics in the Middle Ages*. Madison, WI: University of Wisconsin Press.

Cook. John W. (1979), 'A reappraisal of Leibniz's views on space, time, and motion', reprinted in Woolhouse 1994, vol. 3, pp. 20–61, from *Philosophical Investigations*, 2, 22–63.

Cottingham, John, *et al.* (1970), *The Philosophical Writings of Descartes*, 2 vols. Cambridge: Cambridge University Press.

Couturat, Louis (1902), 'On Leibniz's metaphysics', reprinted in Woolhouse 1994, vol. 1, pp. 1–19, from Frankfurt 1972, pp. 19–45.

Curley, E. M. (1972), 'The root of contingency', reprinted in Woolhouse 1994, vol. 1, pp. 187–207, from Frankfurt 1972, pp. 69–97.

Dijksterhuis, E. J. (1961), *The Mechanization of the World Picture*. Oxford: Oxford University Press.

Dugas, René (1958), *Mechanics in the Seventeenth Century*. Neuchâtel-Switzerland: Éditions du Griffon.

Fleming, Noel (1987), 'On Leibniz on subject and substance', reprinted in Woolhouse 1994, vol. 2, pp. 105–27, from *Philosophical Review*, 96, 69–95.

Frankel, Lois (1981), 'Leibniz's principle of the identity of indiscernibles', reprinted in Woolhouse 1994, vol. 3, pp. 127–47, from *Studia Leibnitiana*, 13, 192–211.

—— (1984), 'Being able to do otherwise: Leibniz on freedom and contingency', reprinted in Woolhouse 1994, vol. 4, pp. 284–302, from *Studia Leibnitiana* 15, 45–59.

—— (1986), 'From a metaphysical point of view: Leibniz and the principle of sufficient reason', reprinted in Woolhouse 1994, vol. 1, pp. 58–73, from *Southern Journal of Philosophy*, 24, 321–33.

Furth, Montgomery (1967), 'Monadology', reprinted in Woolhouse 1994, vol. 4, pp. 2–27, from *Philosophical Review*, 76, 169–200.

Gale, George (1976), 'On what God choose: Perfection and God's freedom', *Studia Leibnitiana*, 8, 69–87.

Garber, Daniel (1983), 'Mind, body and the laws of nature in Descartes and Leibniz', in Peter French *et al.* (eds), *Midwest Studies in Philosophy*, 8, 105–33.

—— (1986), 'Leibniz and the foundations of physics: The middle years', in Kathleen Okruhlik and James Brown (eds), *The Natural Philosophy of Leibniz*. Dordrecht: Reidel, pp. 27–130.

—— (1995), 'Leibniz: Physics and philosophy', in Jolley 1995, pp. 270–352.

—— (1996) 'Review of Robert Merrihew Adams's *Leibniz: determinist, theist, idealist*', *Leibniz Society Review*, 6, 89–106.

Gassendi, Pierre (1644), *Rebuttals Concerning the Metaphysics of René Descartes*, in Craig B. Brush (trans. and ed.) (1972) *The Selected Works of Pierre Gassendi*. New York and London: Johnson Reprint.

Gotterbarn, Donald (1976), 'Leibniz's completion of Descartes's proof', *Studia Leibnitiana*, 8, 105–12.

Greenberg, Sean (2005), 'Leibniz against Molinism: Freedom, indifference, and the nature of the will', in Rutherford and Cover 2005, pp. 217–33.

Hall, Marie Boas (1960), 'The machinery of nature', in A. R. Hall (ed.), *The Making of Modern Science*. Leicester: Leicester University Press, pp. 31–8.

Hanfling, Oswald (1981), 'Leibniz's principle of reason', reprinted in Woolhouse 1994, vol. 1, pp. 74–81, from *Studia Leibnitiana*, Sonderheft 9, 67–73.

Hartz, Glenn (1998), 'Why corporeal substances keep popping up in Leibniz's later philosophy', *British Journal for the History of Philosophy*, 6, 193–207.

Hartz, Glenn A. and Cover, J. A. (1988), 'Space and time in the Leibnizian metaphysic', reprinted in Woolhouse 1994, vol. 3, pp. 76–103, from *Noûs*, 22, 493–519.

Hirschmann, David (1988), 'The kingdom of wisdom and the kingdom of power in Leibniz', reprinted in Woolhouse 1994, vol. 3, pp. 380–9, from *Proceedings of the Aristotelian Society*, 88, 147–59.

Hostler, John (1975), *Leibniz's Moral Philosophy*. London: Duckworth.

Hume, David (1779), in Martin Bell (ed.) (1990) *David Hume Dialogues concerning Natural Religion*. London: Penguin.

Iltis, Carolyn (1971), 'Leibniz and the *vis viva* controversy', *Isis*, 62, 21–35.

—— (1973a) 'The decline of Cartesianism in mechanics: The Leibnizian-Cartesian debates', *Isis*, 64, 356–73.

—— (1973b), 'The Leibnizian-Newtonian debates: Natural philosophy and social psychology', *British Journal for the History of Science*, 6, 343–77.

Ishiguro, Hidé (1977), 'Pre-established harmony *versus* constant conjunction: A reconsideration of the distinction between rationalism and empiricism', reprinted in Woolhouse 1994, vol. 3, pp. 399–420, from *Proceedings of the British Academy*, 63, 239–63.

—— (1979a), 'Contingent truths and possible worlds', reprinted in Woolhouse 1981, pp. 64–76, from *Midwest Studies in Philosophy*, 4, 357–67.

—— (1979b), 'Substances and individual notions', reprinted in Woolhouse 1994, vol. 2, pp. 128–40, from E. Sosa (ed.), *The Philosophy of Nicholas Rescher*. Dordrecht: Reidel, pp. 125–37.

Jarrett, Charles E. (1978), 'Leibniz on truth and contingency', reprinted in Woolhouse 1994, vol. 1, pp. 97–113, from *Canadian Journal of Philosophy*, supplement 4, 83–100.

Johnson, Oliver A. (1954), 'Human freedom in the best of all possible worlds', *Philosophical Quarterly*, 4, 147–55.

Jolley, Nicholas (1986), 'Leibniz and phenomenalism', reprinted in Woolhouse 1994, vol. 4, pp. 150–67, from *Studia Leibnitiana*, 18, 38–51.

—— (ed.) (1995), *The Cambridge Companion to Leibniz*. New York: Cambridge University Press.

—— (2005), 'Leibniz and occasionalism', in Rutherford and Cover 2005, pp. 121–34.

Kant, Immanuel (1781/1787) in Norman Kemp Smith (trans.) (1958) *Immanuel Kant's Critique of Pure Reason*. London: Macmillan.)

—— (1804), 'What real progress has metaphysics made?', in Paul Guyer and Allen W. Wood (eds) (2002), *The Cambridge Edition of the Works of Immanuel Kant: Theoretical Philosophy after 1781*. Cambridge: Cambridge University Press.

Kenny, Anthony (trans. and ed.) (1970), *Descartes: Philosophical Letters*. Oxford: Oxford University Press.

Kulstad, Mark (1983), 'Leibniz on consciousness and reflection', reprinted in Woolhouse 1994, vol. 4, pp. 28–59, from *Southern Journal of Philosophy*, supplement 21, 39–65.

Lactantius (313), *De ira dei* in Mary Francis McDonald (1965), *Lactantius: The Minor Works*. Washington, DC: Catholic University of America Press.

La Forge, Louis de (1666), *Traité de l'esprit de l'homme*, in Pierre Clair (ed.) (1974), *Louis de la Forge (1632–1666): Oeuvres philosophiques*. Paris: Presses Universitaires de France.

Langley, Alfred Gideon (trans.) (1949), *New Essays Concerning Human Understanding by G. W. Leibniz, together with an Appendix Consisting of Some of his Shorter Pieces*. La Salle, IL.: Open Court.

Latta, Robert (trans.) (1898), *Leibniz: The Monadology and Other Philosophical Writings*. London: Oxford University Press.

Leibniz, G. W. (1686), *Discourse on Metaphysics*, in R. N. D Martin and Stuart Brown (trans. and eds) (1988), *G. W. Leibniz: Discourse on Metaphysics and Related Writings*. Manchester: Manchester University Press.

—— (1686–1690), Correspondence with Arnauld. References are to the page numbers (as given in Mason and Parkinson 1967) of the French text in vol. 2 of C. I. Gerhardt (ed.) (1849–1863), *Die philosophischen Schriften von Gottfried Wilhelm Leibniz*. 7 vols. Berlin. Where possible, translations are from Woolhouse and Francks 1998, pp. 94–138, otherwise they are my own.

—— (1695), 'New system of the nature of substances', in Woolhouse and Francks 1997, pp. 10–20.

—— (1698), 'On nature itself', in Ariew and Garber 1989, pp. 155–67, cited by paragraph.

—— (1703–1705), 'New essays on human understanding', in Peter Remnant and Jonathan Bennett (trans. and eds) (1981), *G. W. Leibniz: New Essays on Human Understanding*. Cambridge: Cambridge University Press.

—— (1710), *Theodicy*, in Austin Farrer and E. M. Huggard (trans. and eds) (1951), *G. W. Leibniz: Theodicy*. London: Routledge and Kegan Paul.

—— (1714a), *Principles of Nature and Grace*, in Parkinson and Morris 1973, pp. 195–204.

—— (1714b), *Monadology*, in Latta 1898 as revised by Rutherford 1997.

—— (1715–1716), Correspondence with Clarke, in H. G. Alexander (ed.) (1956), *The Leibniz-Clarke Correspondence*. Manchester: Manchester University Press.

Locke, John (1690), in Roger Woolhouse (ed.) (1997), *John Locke: An Essay Concerning Human Understanding*. London: Penguin.

Loeb, Louis (1981), *From Descartes to Hume*. Ithaca, NY: Cornell University Press.

Loemker, Leroy E. (ed.) (1969), *Gottfried Wilhelm Leibniz: Philosophical Papers and Letters*, 2nd ed. Dordrecht: Kluwer.

Lomansky, Loren E. (1970), 'Leibniz and the modal argument for God's existence', *Monist*, 54, 250–69.

MacDonald Ross, George (1984), 'Leibniz's phenomenalism and the construction of matter', reprinted in Woolhouse 1994, vol. 4, pp. 173–86, from *Studia Leibnitiana*, Sonderheft 13, 26–36.

Malebranche, Nicolas (1674–1675), *The Search After Truth*, Thomas M. Lennon and Paul J. Olscamp (trans. and eds) (1980). Columbus, OH: Ohio State University Press.

—— (1677–1678), *Elucidations of the Search After Truth*, Thomas M. Lennon and Paul J. Olscamp (trans. and eds) (1980). Columbus, OH: Ohio State University Press.

—— (1688), *Dialogues on Metaphysics*, Willis Doney (trans.) (1980). New York: Abaris Books.

Mason, H. T. and Parkinson, G. H. R. (1967), *The Leibniz-Arnauld Correspondence*. Manchester: Manchester University Press.

Mates, Benson (1986), *The Philosophy of Leibniz: Metaphysics and Language*. Oxford: Oxford University Press.

McLaughlin, Peter (1993), 'Descartes on mind-body interaction and the conservation of motion', *The Philosophical Review*, 102, 155–82.

McRae, Robert (1976), *Leibniz: Perception, Apperception, and Thought*. Toronto: University of Toronto Press.

—— (1985), 'Miracles and laws', reprinted in Woolhouse 1994, vol. 3, pp. 390–98, from K. Okruhlik and J. R. Brown (1985), *The Natural Philosophy of Leibniz*. Dordrecht: Reidel, pp. 171–81.

Meijering, Theo (1978), 'On contingency in Leibniz's philosophy', *Studia Leibnitiana*, 10, 22–59.

Mercer, Christia (2001), *Leibniz's Metaphysics: Its Origins and Development*. Cambridge: Cambridge University Press.

——, and Sleigh, R. C. Jr. (1995), 'Metaphysics: The early period to the *Discourse on Metaphysics*', in Jolley 1995, pp. 67–123.

Murray, Michael J. (2005), 'Spontaneity and freedom in Leibniz', in Rutherford and Cover 2005, pp. 194–216.

Nadler, Steven (ed.) (1993), *Causation in Early Modern Philosophy*. University Park: Pennsylvania State University.

Nason, John W. (1942), 'Leibniz and the logical argument for individual substances', reprinted in Woolhouse 1981, pp. 11–29, from *Mind*, 51, 201–2.

—— (1946), 'Leibniz's attack on the Cartesian doctrine of extension', *Journal of the History of Ideas*, 7, 447–83.

O'Neill, Eileen (1993), '*Influxus Physicus*' in Nadler 1993, pp. 27–55.

Paley, William (1802), *Natural Theology*. London: Wilks and Taylor for R. Faulder.

Papineau, David (1977), 'The *vis viva* controversy: Do meanings matter?', in Woolhouse 1994, vol. 3, pp. 198–216, reprinted from *Studies in History and Philosophy of Science*, 8, 111–41.

Parkinson, G. H. R. (1965), *Logic and Reality in Leibniz's Metaphysics*. Oxford: Oxford University Press.

—— (1970), 'Leibniz on human freedom', *Studia Leibnitiana*, Sonderheft 2, 1–67.

—— (1982), 'The "intellectualisation of appearances": Aspects of Leibniz's theory of sensation and thought', reprinted in Woolhouse 1994, vol. 4, pp. 67–86, from Michael Hooker (ed.) (1982), *Leibniz: Critical and Interpretive Essays*. Minneapolis, MN: University of Minnesota Press, pp. 3–20.

—— and Morris, Mary (trans. and eds) (1973), *Leibniz: Philosophical Writings*. London: Dent.

Phemister, Pauline (1991), 'Leibniz, freedom of will and rationality', *Studia Leibnitiana*, 23, 25–39.

Rescher, Nicholas (1967), *The Philosophy of Leibniz*. Englewood Cliffs, NJ: Prentice Hall.

—— (1969), 'Logical difficulties in Leibniz's metaphysics', reprinted in Woolhouse 1994, vol. 2, pp. 176–86, from Nicholas Rescher, *Essays in Philosophical Analysis*. Pittsburgh, PA: University of Pittsburgh Press.

—— (1979), *Leibniz: An Introduction to His Philosophy*. Oxford: Basil Blackwell.

—— (1981), *Leibniz's Metaphysics of Nature*. Dordrecht: Reidel.

Resnik, Lawrence (1973), 'God and the best possible world', *American Philosophical Quarterly*, 10, 313–17.

Russell, Bertrand (1900), *A Critical Exposition of the Philosophy of Leibniz*. London: Allen and Unwin.

Rutherford, Donald (1993), 'Natures, laws and miracles: The roots of Leibniz's critique of occasionalism', in Nadler 1993, pp. 135–8.

—— (1995a), *Leibniz and the Rational Order of Nature*. Cambridge: Cambridge University Press.

—— (1995b), 'Metaphysics: The late period', in Jolley 1995, pp. 124–75.

—— (1997), Revised translation of Latta 1898, at http://philosophy.ucsd.edu/faculty/rutherford/Leibniz/monad.htm

—— (2005), 'Leibniz on spontaneity', in Rutherford and Cover 2005, pp. 156–80.

—— and Cover, J. A. (eds) (2005), *Leibniz: Nature and Freedom*. Oxford: Oxford University Press.

Savile, Anthony (2000), *Leibniz and the 'Monadology'*. London: Routledge.

Sergeant, John (1697), *Solid Philosophy Asserted*. London.

Sleigh, R. C., Jr. (1983), 'Leibniz on the two great principles of all our reasonings', reprinted in Woolhouse 1994, vol. 1, pp. 31–57, from *Midwest Studies in Philosophy*, 8, 193–215.

—— (1990a), *Leibniz and Arnauld: A Commentary on Their Correspondence*. New Haven, CT: Yale University Press.

—— (1990b), 'Leibniz on Malebranche on causality', in J. A. Cover and Mark Kulstad (eds), *Central Themes in Early Modern Philosophy*. Indianapolis, IN: Hackett, pp. 161–93.

Toland, John (1704), *Letters to Serena*. London (reprinted 1964, Stuttgart: Frommann).

Tournemine, René Joseph (1703), 'Conjectures on the union of the soul and the body', in Woolhouse and Francks 1997, pp. 247–9.

Vailati, Ezio (1986), 'Leibniz on necessary and contingent predication', reprinted in Woolhouse 1994, vol. 1, pp. 330–49, from *Studia Leibnitiana*, 18, 195–210.

Vinci, Thomas C. (1974), 'What is the ground for the principle of the identity of indiscernibles in the Leibniz-Clarke correspondence?', *Journal of the History of Philosophy*, 12, 95–101.

Voltaire (1758), *Candide or Optimism*, trans. John Butt (1947). Harmondsworth: Penguin Books.

Westfall, Richard F. (1971), *Force in Newton's Physics: The Science of Dynamics in the Seventeenth Century*. London: Macdonald.

Wiggins, David (1987), 'The concept of the subject contains the concept of the predicate', reprinted in Woolhouse 1994, vol. 2, pp. 141–63, from Judith Jarvis Thompson (ed.) (1987) *On Being and Saying: Essays for Richard Cartwright*. Cambridge, MA: MIT Press, pp. 263–84.

Wilson, Catherine (1982), Leibniz and atomism', reprinted in Woolhouse 1994, vol. 3, pp. 342–68, from *Studies in History and Philosophy of Science*, 13, 175–99.

—— (1983), 'Leibnizian optimism', reprinted in Woolhouse 1994, vol. 4, pp. 433–50, from *The Journal of Philosophy*, 80, 765–83.

—— (1989), *Leibniz's Metaphysics: A Historical and Comparative Study*. Princeton, NJ: Princeton University Press.

Wilson, Margaret D. (1987), 'The phenomenalisms of Leibniz and Berkeley', in E. Sosa (ed.) (1987), *Essays on the Philosophy of George Berkeley*. Dordrecht: Reidel, pp. 3–22.

Wilson, N. L. (1973), 'Individual identity, space, and time in the Leibniz-Clarke correspondence', in I. Leclerc (ed.), *The Philosophy of Leibniz and the Modern World*. Nashville, TN: Vanderbilt University Press, pp. 189–206.

Winterbourne, A. T. (1982), 'On the metaphysics of Leibnizian space and time', reprinted in Woolhouse 1994, vol. 3, pp. 62–75, from *Studies in the History and Philosophy of Science*, 13, 201–14.

Woolhouse, R. S. (ed.) (1981), *Leibniz: Metaphysics and Philosophy of Science*. Oxford: Oxford University Press.

—— (1983), *Locke*. Brighton: Harvester Press.

—— (1985), 'Pre-established harmony retuned: Ishiguro *versus* the tradition', *Studia Leibnitiana*, 17, 204–19.

—— (ed.) (1994), *Gottfried Wilhelm Leibniz: Critical Assessments*, 4 vols. London: Routledge.

—— (2000), 'Pre-established harmony between soul and body: union or unity?', in A. Lamarra and R. Palaia (eds), *Unità e Molteplicità nel Pensiero Filosofico e Scientificio di Leibniz*. Firenze: Olschki, pp. 159–70.

—— and Richard Francks (trans. and eds) (1997), *Leibniz's 'New System', and Associated Contemporary Texts*. Oxford: Oxford University Press.

—— and Richard Francks (trans. and eds) (1998), *G. W. Leibniz: Philosophical Texts*. Oxford: Oxford University Press.

INDEX